Essay
Writing Skills

Essay
Writing Skills

Essential techniques to
gain top grades

Jacqueline Connelly
and Patrick Forsyth

KoganPage

LONDON PHILADELPHIA NEW DELHI

Publisher's note

Every possible effort has been made to ensure that the information contained in this book is accurate at the time of going to press, and the publishers and authors cannot accept responsibility for any errors or omissions, however caused. No responsibility for loss or damage occasioned to any person acting, or refraining from action, as a result of the material in this publication can be accepted by the editor, the publisher or either of the authors.

First published in Great Britain and the United States in 2011 by Kogan Page Limited

120 Pentonville Road	1518 Walnut Street, Suite 1100	4737/23 Ansari Road
London N1 9JN	Philadelphia PA 19102	Daryaganj
United Kingdom	USA	New Delhi 110002
www.koganpage.com		India

© Jacqueline Connelly and Patrick Forsyth, 2012

The right of Jacqueline Connelly and Patrick Forsyth to be identified as the authors of this work has been asserted by them in accordance with the Copyright, Designs and Patents Act 1988.

ISBN   978 0 7494 6391 5
E-ISBN   978 0 7494 6392 2

British Library Cataloguing-in-Publication Data

A CIP record for this book is available from the British Library.

Library of Congress Cataloging-in-Publication Data

Forsyth, Patrick B.
   Essay writing skills : essential techniques to gain top marks / Patrick Forsyth,
Jacqueline Connelly.
      p. cm.
   Includes bibliographical references.
   ISBN 978-0-7494-6391-5 – ISBN 978-0-7494-6392-2   1. Essay–Authorship.
2. English language–Rhetoric.   I. Connelly, Jacqueline.   II. Title.
   PN4500.F67 2012
   808.4–dc23
                                                                    2011043141

Typeset by Graphicraft Limited, Hong Kong
Printed and bound in India by Replika Press Pvt Ltd

*For Fabian and Tilly – some more information
to help you get ahead one day*

Contents

Foreword

It's easy to regard writing academic essays as a chore. You simply cannot afford to do that. Essay writing is an essential part of every degree programme. Both the coursework and examination assessment elements of degree programmes usually require essays regardless of the discipline being studied. Some degree programmes, particularly those in the Arts and Humanities, use the essay as the crucial unit of assessment. In short, you won't get a good degree result unless you master the art of the essay. Completing a good essay requires a broad range of skills, which is why so many degree programmes build them into their assessment patterns. A good essay demands that a student shows the ability to plan, time-manage, research, summarize and develop cohesive and balanced arguments before reaching clear, concise conclusions. Therefore a good essay, once completed, is actually a mini academic masterclass in its own right: it is the essence of the intellectual demands of a degree programme. It is the distillation of the philosopher Francis Bacon's (1561–1626) dictum that, 'Reading maketh a full man; conference a ready man; and writing an exact man.'

Essays at the university level provide a very different challenge to that experienced in all earlier forms of study. Most first-year students experience a feeling of dread when they are handed their module outlines containing the set essay questions. The questions are undoubtedly demanding as they are designed to stretch your intellect to its limits. This does not mean that essay writing is deliberately designed to be an intimidating experience. Universities set you an intellectual challenge in the essays. You should therefore regard the essay as a compliment. In effect, your lecturers are inviting you to take the first steps towards joining them. They are revealing their confidence in your ability to rise to the challenge. You should therefore look at essays as the stage on which to show off your growing skills and knowledge.

Mastering essay writing also provides a highly valuable transferable skill. In an information-driven economy the ability to evaluate, interpret and process fluently information drawn from a range of sources – all of which are demanded by essay writing – reveals a candidate with a flexible and incisive mind.

Universities provide much support for students. This is often both generic and programme-specific. This guide helps contextualize and complement that information. Working through a range of approaches it will show you how to deal with essay questions by breaking down the process into a series of steps. Following these steps will help you demystify that challenge. It will help you understand that the essay should not be viewed as something awful to be avoided for as long as possible, but an enriching and enjoyable challenge that will allow you the power to express to the full the fruits of your research, shaped and moulded by your ideas.

Few experiences at university match the satisfaction of completing a good essay. Receiving an essay back from a marker who has clearly appreciated the work that has gone into it and has rewarded it accordingly can leave an intense sense of pride in a job well done. A good essay bolsters the confidence, provides the basis for revision and is an obvious sign that the intellectual aims of the programme have been understood. With the help of this book, and the kind of approaches it commends, good essays are exactly what you will produce.

Mark Connelly
Professor of Modern British History
University of Kent

The authors wish to thank Mark Connelly, not only for writing the Foreword but also for his help throughout the writing of this book. His experience and particularly his experience with many students currently and in the past has informed the project and allowed it to reflect the real questions and concerns typically expressed by students getting to grips with the university environment and the challenge of essay writing.

Introduction: destination graduation

This introduction makes clear why you need good essay-writing skills, how they can benefit you and how they fit into the whole picture of your ongoing study, at whatever stage of this you may be. The book will help you direct your efforts so that, amongst a tall pile of essays awaiting marking, yours will be read by your lecturer with pleasure.

Like our earlier title, *The Study Skills Guide – Essential strategies for smart students*, this book is designed to provide practical advice that is manageable to implement and which will make it more likely that you will graduate successfully. In the earlier book a wide canvass of issues was reviewed to examine and promote a whole range of necessary actions that will allow a student to excel. The focus in this volume is narrow and specific. It is on the effective writing of essays that forms such an important task during so many courses and also in the exams that go with them, indeed which can be a major influence on results and grades. But its context is similar: the need to get the most from time spent in any sort of higher or further education establishment. So we start by reiterating something of what was said in the Introduction to the earlier volume; such points have been made more important recently with changes coming to the funding and cost of higher education.

If you are reading this you are likely to be approaching or have just taken a big step: moving into higher or further education. If so, then however you got there, either straight from school or going back to education as a mature student in the middle of your career or after a spell in work, it is doubtless an achievement. You have been accepted onto a course at a higher or further education institution with the intention of getting a degree or other qualification.

New realities

If you are at this stage, or contemplating it, make no mistake: life is going to change and maybe change radically. University or college is not like school. Certainly it is much less regimented and there is less supervision and that may sound good, but it leaves much more down to you. You need to adapt to new ways of working, fit with new systems and procedures and find ways of doing so that meet the need and yet suit you. There may well be other significant changes that go with the move. Many people move to a new area, many find themselves living away from home for the first time and some find all that takes a bit of getting used to. So be it. Things are going to be different and finding somewhere to live and sorting out your finances take time. You may be juggling university work with family commitments.

But most people find all this readjustment eminently worthwhile. It is a stage when your whole way of life changes: new places, new people and new things to do, and above all a new freedom – the period ahead should be interesting, it should be enjoyable and it puts you on a path that can potentially influence the rest of your life – enabling you to start to fulfil your ambitions and carve out the future life you want.

You may face changes, but you are also presented with a major opportunity. Yes, major: higher education is the life and career equivalent of an open goal. But it does not just happen: you must make the most of it. Opportunities need grasping. In this book we focus not so much on making your next few years fun (though there is every reason why they should be just that) but rather on helping you ensure that you can tackle the essay-writing element of your work in a way that is manageable, stress-free and most likely to ensure you succeed in getting the result you want.

(Note: while there is a whole range of institutions, from a variety of further education colleges to universities, including specialist institutions such as business and medical schools, the word 'university' is used here to include them all. The type of essay that we consider in this book is that which students in higher education will need to write. However, much of what we say will be relevant and useful to students in further education as well.)

Here is a key question to ask: *will you graduate successfully and with the degree classification that you want?* There is every likelihood that you will, but this will only be the case if you get to grips with, and work with, a new situation. Doing so requires understanding, consideration and application; this makes the process sound like hard work and surely your course itself will be hard work enough. This book aims to streamline the process of essay writing: to kick-start you into a new, effective and appropriate way of preparing and executing written work that will help make it easier and increase your chances of success both day-by-day and in terms of your ultimate graduation.

This applies whatever the nature of what you study. You may be studying to obtain a non-vocational qualification; for instance subjects such as business administration or marketing could take you into a wide range of business careers. Indeed your chosen subject may, at this stage, be more general still and linking it to a specific career choice may be another decision to be made over the next few years. Alternatively, you may be studying to gain a vocational or professional qualification, perhaps one linked to a specific career choice already made. To be a doctor, a research scientist, computer designer or whatever may necessitate particular qualifications being obtained. Doing so is simply a given if you are to pursue your chosen path.

The approaches reviewed here are all necessary, practical and manageable. What may initially seem in some ways simple can be problematical, so taking your essay writing seriously is important for several reasons:

- Primarily, essay writing and all that it involves are essential for developing a range of academic skills that you will need to succeed in your course.

- Good, well-marked essays provide the stepping stones that take you towards a good result, a degree or qualification.

- Writing your essay in a serious and thus systematic way, one designed to accurately reflect the brief and score good marks, will also allow you to complete the task more quickly than will an ad hoc approach.

- Essay writing also has a direct effect on learning. Psychologists tell us that learning is reinforced and made more permanent if things are written down; the act of writing actually prompts the brain to remember and do so more easily. If your studies demand the storing of facts and information, this is a useful side effect of essay writing and of the research and preparation that precedes it.

- The skills that make for good essay writing can also form the basis of more broad-based writing skills that are useful in a whole variety of ways, both during your course and beyond in the wider world, not least in terms of your career (more of this later).

Getting on top of the whole study process is vital. Keep up to date, maximize the use of your time, work in an effective and disciplined way and you will work successfully and have time for the other things you want to do. Get behind, or waste time and catching up becomes difficult, achieving the results you want becomes less likely and the problem escalates as time available to catch up is limited; there will also be a real clash between work and your social or home life. Good essay-writing technique is an important part of this whole process and getting on top of that can help disproportionately in your search for good grades.

Future realities

There is a further broad point to keep in mind here. The world, and the world of work specifically, have changed a great deal in recent years. It is a safe prediction that it will change more and is likely to change more quickly.

The world of work is dynamic and competitive. Employers have had to contend with volatile economies and operating conditions. In the commercial sector, competition for jobs (and promotion) is as fierce as it has ever been. Organizations only succeed if their employees have the necessary skills and experience and perform well at whatever they may do. They know this. Thus careful recruitment and selection are regarded as vital, not least because employment legislation has made mistakes (employing someone who proves inadequate and must be replaced) an expensive and time-consuming process to correct.

All this means that even those with the best qualifications do not necessarily just walk straight out of higher education into the job they want. Sadly you are unlikely to work magic just by snapping your fingers and saying 'Hire me'. You will need to work at job-seeking in due course, and then at ongoing career management. Thus every aspect of your record during higher education can help create for you a profile that appeals to employers. You want to gain the qualification you aim at, you want to achieve that with an impressive record of how you have spent the time leading up to it, and you want to do all this in a manageable way that allows you to benefit from and enjoy the whole process.

Effective writing is not solely a necessary exercise to be done as part of study, it is a career skill: one worth cultivating because it can help you towards good grades and then form the foundation of a skill much valued in the workplace. Everything you are trying to get to grips with here may seem something of a chore, but remember the old saying that the only place where success comes before work is in the dictionary. In fact getting to grips with everything here is doubly worth the effort as it will not only benefit you during your time at university, but will be valuable both in the transition – the move from education to work – and in your work career.

This seems so important that Chapter 7 explores the situation and the opportunity it presents in more detail, looking at three main areas. First is using your writing skills to help you create and enhance the documentation – CVs and more – that aims to obtain you the job you want. Second is using your writing achievements as part of your record of achievement, and third is how such skills assist in your career.

Just as we were writing this introduction a headline appeared, big, bold and top of the front page on the *Daily Telegraph*. It read: 'Pupils Will Lose Marks for Poor Grammar and Spelling'. In the article that followed the chairman of Marks & Spencer was quoted as suggesting that too many of those applying for jobs 'are not fit for work'. Along with adequate numeracy, communication skills, including writing skills, were high on the list of what he meant. If you want a prediction, it seems to us that this headline may well mark a turning point: such things are likely to grow in importance across education as a whole, so be warned. Note too that grammar and spelling are just one small part of what is necessary if you are to write a good essay – as we will see.

This book aims to smooth the path. Whether you are just starting, or indeed are a little way down the track, the lessons here can help you achieve what you want and increase the likelihood that you can excel.

How to use this book

To get the best from reading this book it is worth keeping pen and paper close at hand:

- Note when anything mentioned seems to have direct application for you.

- Record any specific action you will take (even if this is simply to consider something further).

- Watch for 'Action boxes' within the text; these are designed to help point the way, creating links to your own situation.

- Use the 'Your notes' pages at the end of each chapter.

- Make the book 'yours' by adding notes, coupled perhaps with highlighting key parts of the text; turn the book into your personal guide to the task ahead, one that will be useful throughout your course.

Act now! Be warned: time starts to go quickly once you are into higher or further education, and there are many distractions, some constructive, others not. There is a line written by John Lennon which says that life is what happens while you are busy making other plans. It's a sobering thought. It is all too easy to find you are a substantial way through your chosen course and lagging behind what you intended, and having to take emergency remedial action midway can – even if it is effective –

dilute the satisfaction to be gained from the whole process. A little time spent now will ensure that your first thought on graduation day does not start with the words, 'If only ...'.

So let's see how you can work smarter, not harder, and make your essay-writing skills a real asset now and in the future.

Your notes

....

....

....

....

....

....

....

....

....

....

....

....

....

....

....

....

....

....

....

....

....

....

CHAPTER 1

The academic essay: its nature and role

In this chapter we look at the nature of the essay, and what distinguishes it from other forms of writing. As part of this we consider the rules and conventions that apply to essay writing and the reasons why essays are a critical part of your course.

What is an essay?

Most further and higher education courses will require you to write essays. Indeed if you are reading this book then we can assume that yours does too. Such essays are likely to be the most significant individual piece of work you will have attempted in your education to date. Essays are significant in:

● their length – an essay is unlikely to have fewer than 1,500 words and may have as many as 2,500; some courses allow 'double essays' of up to 5,000 words;

● the time required to complete them;

● the outcome – the grade you receive is likely to contribute to the final outcome of your course;

● and finally, most important, the intellectual application required.

Essays are not, therefore, something that you will be able to do well without considerable planning and preparation.

As essay is a piece of writing that attempts to explore in detail a particular subject. It is not the only form of writing that does this. We could consider that newspaper and magazine articles, and guidebooks, for example, also have the same purpose. However, three things distinguish the essay from other writing forms:

1 An essay is a formal piece of writing and as such it has certain **conventions**. Many of these will be implicit and not be spelt out in detail by your lecturers; you will be expected to be aware of them. It is critically important that you understand this. You are not being asked to jot down your personal views in an ad hoc manner, but to demonstrate your knowledge and skills in a very specific way.

2 Even more important, an essay, at least in the context that we are discussing in this book, is a piece of **assessed coursework**. It is a way for your lecturers to judge your progress and understanding and to give you a grade or mark accordingly. You will be writing it in response to a particular question set for you (or, usually, a list of questions from which you will select one), not randomly, but very carefully to test your knowledge and skills.

3 As well as being used to assess you, writing essays is used by your lecturers to **develop your academic skills** by allowing you to:
   - explore a particular topic in great detail (much greater than lectures or seminars do);
   - consider the academic debate on the subject;
   - reflect on this debate and the facts you uncover to develop your own views;
   - improve your reading and writing skills.

Below, we consider each of these points in a little more detail. However, before we do so it is important that you understand what an essay represents for you. It is an opportunity: an opportunity for you to display the extent of your understanding of the subject, the breadth and depth of your background research and your command of the wider subject matter.

On the other hand nothing will expose your lack of knowledge more completely than a poor essay. Nothing in this book is going to help you write a good essay if you haven't done the appropriate background research first (see Chapter 3 for advice on how to approach this). What this book can do is help you understand what is required of you, how to go about this research, and how to put your essay together to meet the expectations.

Essay conventions

Like many forms of specialist writing, essay writing has a set of conventions that you need to follow when completing your coursework. Failing to follow these conventions will have implications not just on the grade you will receive, but on how you and your abilities are perceived and, perhaps most important, on the extent to which you develop your own academic skills through the essay-writing process. These conventions include the following.

Formal language and presentation

The style of writing you need to use for essays and other academic writing is very different from the style you use elsewhere. It is much more formal than e-mails and letters. This means that you must:

- Avoid slang, colloquial terms, clichés and abbreviations (this means not using 'they're' and 'weren't' or such terms as 'eg' and 'ie') though, as with everything in this list, check for 'local' requirements and practice.

- Use full sentences; bullet point lists are not acceptable for essays (as distinct from a book like this where such things are almost mandatory to ensure a quick and easy read for busy people).

- Use correct grammar and spelling. This is important. You will not impress your lecturers if you misspell key technical information in your field. Poor grammar and spelling are inexcusable and give an overall sloppy impression (see Chapter 2 for more detailed guidance on this area).

- Avoid the use of 'I'. Instead use phrases such as 'As has been demonstrated above ...', 'The next point to consider is ...' and so on.

- Avoid subjective language such as 'excellent', 'awful', 'bad', 'pretty' and so on. Try to be objective in your writing.

Almost all essays are written using a computer, which certainly makes it easier to present it well; so with several years of writing ahead it may be worth working on improving your typing skills and adapting them for the task of academic writing. Detail is important; you should:

- Avoid using a variety of different fonts, sizes and styles throughout, which looks messy and can be hard to read.

- Use bold, italics and underlining to highlight headings (if used) or key points only where necessary, and avoid overusing them.

- Most important, make sure you follow any guidance from your lecturer about how he or she wants the essay presented.

A clear line of argument, which develops through the piece

Your essay will address a question or topic, usually set by your lecturers. You need not only to research and summarize the disparate views on the topic, but also to develop and set out your own understanding and opinion. Your essay should then develop your argument progressively, through both its structure and content, with a logical line of reasoning and clear conclusions.

At this point it is also worth stressing the importance of relevance. Your essay must:

- cover what is required;

- be free of irrelevant content or digression.

Comprehensiveness is *never* an objective. If an essay touched on absolutely everything then it would certainly be too long. In fact, you always have to be selective: if you do not say everything, then everything you do say is a choice – you need to make good content choices, and this is one of the skills you need to develop.

Use of evidence to support your argument

At university level it is insufficient to simply state your opinion, or even that of others, so:

- The statements you make in your essays need to be evidenced through referencing other material.

- You will be unable to make a persuasive case or even to answer the question without using material from lectures, books, journal articles, websites and other sources.

- You will need to evaluate and assess this evidence as part of developing your argument.

- You must show that you understand there are other ways to interpret the evidence and try to demonstrate where there are weaknesses in them.

- Be honest: if there are gaps or weaknesses in your own line of reasoning, you must use evidence to show why you still think your conclusions are appropriate.

Clear references

In all essays you need to show the precise source of the information, arguments and ideas you use. This is true whether or not you quote directly from the other work. University-level study demands that you develop your own ideas and critical thinking. It is fundamental to this that you do not try to pass off other people's ideas and arguments as your own (doing this is called plagiarism; see box). Therefore the convention of referencing is used to show where the ideas come from. References should be used when you quote directly from, paraphrase, or even just rely on the information and ideas within another work.

There are other benefits to referencing too. It allows readers to refer back to the source themselves if they wish (and it may be that other readers will interpret the same material differently from you). Using references like this is one way to make your essay persuasive; it shows that you have evidence to back up what you are saying. Using a wide range of well-chosen references will also demonstrate the thoroughness of your research. (More details on how to include references in your essay are included in Chapter 5.)

PLAGIARISM

Plagiarism, or passing off someone else's work as your own, is a major offence (and may also involve breach of copyright and copyright law). It includes:

- quoting or paraphrasing another person's work without acknowledgement;
- using ideas or arguments developed by another without acknowledgement.

Plagiarism is likely to lead to you receiving a zero for the particular essay involved and, if you persist, it could even mean that you are not allowed to continue your course. Lecturers are used to identifying plagiarism in student coursework, however cleverly it is disguised. Many universities require electronic copies of essays to be submitted so that they can be subjected to plagiarism detection software.

You *will* be caught. Don't even think about it!

ACTION

To make sure you can reference other works accurately, and avoid plagiarism, it is important that you keep good notes as you research. As you will need to study a wide range of material you will quickly lose track of which ideas came from where if you are not careful.

Structure

Within these broadly applicable conventions different subjects have different models for essay writing, especially in the sciences. Here is an example essay structure that would be appropriate for most other subjects.

EXAMPLE ESSAY STRUCTURE

Title: The essay title is a key part of the essay itself. Make sure you understand and stick to the question asked.

Introduction: Explore the essay question or title, make your line of argument clear, summarize your conclusion and state briefly the evidence you are going to examine to demonstrate this.

Main part of essay: Here you develop your argument. Break different ideas down into paragraphs, making sure there is a logical sequence from each one to the next, and that overall a persuasive line of reasoning is developed.

Conclusion: Summarize the main ideas in your essay (don't introduce any new ideas at this stage), clearly stating your own conclusions, and showing why these are important.

References: References may be in the form of footnotes throughout the essay, or endnotes. How they are set out and dealt with is very important; see Chapter 5 for more details on the convention of referencing.

Bibliography: Don't make the mistake of thinking this is an extra or add-on section. In subjects where this is used (in some it is not necessary) the bibliography is a core part of the essay. Here you should list all the books, journal articles and other evidence you have consulted in answering the question, even those that you have not taken references from, with the full bibliographic details of each piece in the same format as you have used for references. Order the bibliography alphabetically, using the surname of the author. And beware: do not be tempted to include items that you have not referred to – their content, when compared to your essay, may make it clear that you are bluffing.

Word limit

Whatever type of coursework you are doing there will be a word limit. If a lecturer asks for 2,000 words it is because he or she believes that will allow you to do justice to the subject. Delivering 1,000 or 5,000 is not likely to be well regarded. Keeping to the word limit is one of the skills that essay writing is designed to test you on. You are not, of course, expected to hit the word limit exactly and you can work on the basis of about 10 per cent or so leeway either way, though this can vary somewhat and it is useful to check. Again, this will become easier with practice and may well be largely instinctive after a number of essays.

The essay as assessed coursework

The final grade you will receive for your course is likely to be determined by both examination and coursework. This means that each essay you write will have an impact on this outcome, so it is worth taking the time and trouble to get it as good as you can.

You need to plan carefully in advance of each essay to ensure that:

- You make available the required time (taking lectures, seminars and other classes, as well as other coursework that you may have into account);

- You have all the materials you need to hand when you need them (for example, this means that you need to check whether you will have to recall any essential books that may be out of the library a week or so before you plan to use them).

WHO ARE YOU WRITING FOR?

As a student the essay you write is unlikely to have a wide audience. Its primary purpose is to meet the requirements of your course, and it will be read and assessed by your lecturer. Some essays will be looked at by a second marker, or the external examiner, but all do so with the same purpose in mind: to assess your progress and see how well you have interpreted and answered the question. This will allow them to give you a mark that will feed into your final grade. You may share draft or completed essays with friends (and some universities have essay banks), but you are not writing for them. Keep your audience and purpose in mind as you write.

Your lecturers will be looking for you to display particular academic skills through your essay, and the grade you receive will depend upon how well you do this. It is crucial that you understand what they are looking for at the start of your course and before you begin any essays. It is likely that there will be a handbook or something similar for your course or department that lays this out in detail; make sure that you familiarize yourself with it. As an example we include in Table 1.1 the Essay Classification Descriptors from the Undergraduate Handbook of the School of History at the University of Kent, to whom we are grateful for permission to use this text.

We consider how you display these skills in subsequent chapters of this book. However, at this point, it is important to remember that unless you are studying in this particular department, these are only an example. They are included here to show the kinds of skills that your lecturers will be looking for and to underline the existence

TABLE 1.1

90–100

Outstanding work, brilliantly demonstrating

- A superlative command of the secondary and, where appropriate, primary sources, showing outstanding breadth and depth of knowledge and understanding
- A deep understanding of key concepts
- An exceptional ability to organise, develop and express ideas and arguments in an eloquent and sophisticated manner
- An outstanding capacity for critical analysis and insights
- Striking and sustained originality in argument
- Outstanding ability to engage with, and where appropriate contest, the terms of a question
- Excellent punctuation and spelling
- Immaculate citations and bibliography.

80–89

Exceptional work, impressively demonstrating

- A comprehensive command of secondary and, where appropriate, primary sources, showing exceptional breadth and depth of knowledge and understanding
- An impressive mastery of key concepts
- Impressive ability to organise, develop and express ideas and arguments in a lucid and sophisticated manner
- Highly developed capacity for critical analysis and insights
- Sustained originality in argument
- Impressive ability to see where a question may be problematical
- Excellent punctuation and spelling
- Immaculate citations and bibliography.

70–79

Excellent work, consistently demonstrating

- A thorough command of secondary and, where appropriate, primary sources, showing breadth and depth of knowledge and understanding
- A mastery of key concepts
- An excellent ability to organise, develop and express ideas and arguments in a lucid and sophisticated manner
- Strong capacity for critical analysis and insights
- Some originality in argument
- Ability to see where a question may be problematical
- Excellent punctuation and spelling
- Exactitude in citations and bibliography.

TABLE 1.1 *cont*

60–69

Sound work, demonstrating

- A command of the major secondary and, where appropriate, primary sources, showing some breadth and depth of knowledge and understanding
- An awareness of some key concepts
- A reasonable ability to organise, develop and express relevant ideas and arguments
- Well-structured argument in response to the question
- Clear and grammatically accurate writing
- Reasonably correct citations and bibliography.

50–59

Satisfactory work, demonstrating

- Some partial engagement with the major secondary and, where appropriate, primary sources, indicating adequate knowledge and understanding
- A limited awareness of some key concepts
- A partial ability to organise, develop and express relevant ideas and arguments
- An argument (often descriptive and sometimes lacking focus) in response to the question
- Writing clearly and correctly enough for comprehension despite some errors in punctuation, spelling or syntax
- Fairly regularly incorrect citations and bibliography.

40–49

Weak essays, demonstrating

- Limited engagement with the major secondary and, where appropriate, primary sources, with poor knowledge and understanding
- A very limited awareness of some key concepts
- Sketchiness in response to the question or topic
- Lack of clear focus or direction
- Poor grammar, mispunctuation and/or misuse of words
- Weak use of citations and bibliography.

30–39

Unsatisfactory essays, demonstrating

- Only superficial acquaintance with secondary and, where appropriate, primary sources
- Far less than the expected length
- Lack of coherence in the argument
- Writing rendered nonsensical by errors.

---

of such a document. You need to find the relevant guidelines for your own course and make yourself familiar with them.

Developing your academic skills through essay writing

We have already touched on how significant a piece of work each essay is. This might mean that the process of writing one is daunting for you. However, even if this is so, essay writing is a crucial part of your university learning. You are not required to write essays only to allow your lecturers to assess you, but because it is through the process of researching, drafting and finalizing an essay that you will develop the academic skills that you need to complete your programme successfully. Before we consider the skills that essay writing will help develop, let's think about the support that you can get.

Getting support from lecturers

Your lecturers do not set essays to enjoy watching you suffer. They will be only too pleased to help you if you ask. Don't approach them simply to moan about the volume of work, or the imminence of an impending deadline, especially if the problem is down to your poor planning and time management.

You will find excellent support from them with things like:

- identifying the best way to tackle a problem or piece of coursework from a range of options you present;

- reviewing an early draft;

- checking your writing style is appropriate;

- discussing ideas and questions for essays;

- giving added guidance about suitable reading material.

But you should keep in mind that university is not about spoon-feeding you answers. If that happened, you would not improve your own, independent thinking and analytical skills. What lecturers want to see is that you have been grappling with the issues and now need a bit of advice on the next step.

When you receive your essay back you are likely to have not just a mark, but a cover sheet with a few comments on, detailing the strengths and weaknesses of your essay. (See Chapter 6 of this book where feedback on the example essays included is provided.) In addition to this feedback many lecturers will have specific times when they are available to meet and discuss essays. Don't miss this excellent opportunity for input directly tailored to your work. At such a session:

- Make sure that you understand each comment being made.

- Seek clarification where necessary.

- Ask which were the strong and weak parts of the essay.

- Use their feedback to make sure that you write a better essay next time. (On page 117, we will deal in more detail with how to analyse and act on comments made on your essays.)

As we noted above there are four particular skills that essay writing will help you develop and we shall now look at each in turn:

1. Exploring a particular topic in great detail

A characteristic of university-level study is the breadth and volume of material that you will cover. For example, if you are studying English Literature you may be under-taking four different modules at any one time, each of which requires reading a novel (sometimes a very substantial one) or equivalent each week. You might have one lecture and one seminar on any particular topic. You get a flavour for it, and begin to understand how each topic fits together, but not the opportunity to dig deeper into something that may interest you. The essay gives you just this opportunity. Usually you will be given a list of essay questions to choose from. We shall consider this in more detail in Chapter 3, but it is worth noting here that wherever possible you should choose a question in which you are interested. Writing an essay is a significant piece of work, and if you can do it on a topic that interests you so much the better.

The original material, texts or artefacts about the topic are known as the 'primary sources'. To continue the English Literature example, this would be the novels, plays or other literature; for History of Art it would be paintings, sculptures and so on as well as the personal papers of artists.

You may find that you do not deal directly with primary sources, but this will largely depend on your subject. If you are studying Archaeology then the primary sources may be artefacts from a Roman villa now on display at a museum in Florence, but if you are studying for a degree in some form of Literature then the primary sources are readily available and you will study them directly. Students in History of Art may not be able to gain direct access to all of the relevant artistic works, but they will be able to view very high-quality reproductions. In many subjects you will be required to engage more directly with primary sources in your final year of study and where necessary the relevant materials will be provided.

Whether you engage with the primary sources directly or not, you will need to show a good awareness of the variety of primary sources and their content. However, looking at this material alone is not sufficient; which leads us onto the next point.

2. Consider the academic debate on the subject

The academic debate on a topic is known as the 'secondary sources' (see box below). These are the subsequent studies of the primary sources carried out by academics, and will help you understand the primary sources themselves. These academics won't always agree on their interpretation of the primary sources. For example, one academic may think that one primary source is much older and more significant than another, or there may be a fundamental disagreement about how to interpret a primary source. Writing an essay will require you to become familiar with this debate. Often the debate will have taken place over many years, sometimes hundreds, and you will need to understand how the debate has developed and its current status. You will need to identify whether or not there is any sort of consensus on an issue. You may find that particular academic scholars typify a strand of thinking within such a debate. Often these secondary sources will be listed in your bibliography (see Chapter 5 for more details on what a bibliography is and how to use it), and summarizing their views and possibly quoting key passages will be important in your essay.

As you consider the academic debate you may find scholars whose position you agree with, or others with whom you strongly disagree. This leads us into the next skill being developed by essays, because in addition to an analysis of the primary and secondary sources your own opinion and line of argument need to come through in your essays.

DEFINITION: PRIMARY AND SECONDARY SOURCES

Primary sources are the original materials upon which all interpretations and subsequent studies are based.

Secondary sources are the subsequent studies and interpretations by academics and others over the following years (sometimes many hundreds of years; it is not a primary source just because it is old).

Sources are many and varied and link appropriately to your chosen subject. For example, for an English Literature student primary sources will include novels, poetry and other literature. For a History student they will include diaries, letters and government papers.

---

3. Reflect on this debate and the facts you uncover to develop your own views

At university level your essays are expected not just to survey academic opinion but to begin to evaluate it and make judgements on it. Try to ensure that your essay:

- shows awareness of a range of opinions and arguments;

- deals with these opinions and arguments in a balanced way;

- details where there is room for debate or alternative explanations;

- uses secondary sources and, where appropriate, primary sources;

- has a firm conclusion: make clear which line of argument you favour and give sound and convincing justification for this.

> Remember that an essay is not a statement of your opinion; it is not a tweet, a blog or a fanzine. Whilst carefully researched and informed opinion should form part of your work, this must be within the formal constraints of the essay.

4. Improve your reading and writing skills

We consider writing skills in greater detail in Chapter 2, but reading skills are worth a mention here. You will need to read a large volume of material for any individual essay – the works on the lecturer's bibliography as a minimum. A student with poor reading skills will spend a great deal more time on this than a student with effective reading skills. These come only with practice, but you should be looking to:

- Select which primary and secondary sources are relevant to your essay.

- Quickly identify which parts of the book or article are relevant to your topic (use your bibliography, index, chapter headings (if available) to help).

- Do not be distracted by interesting material that is not relevant; instead make a note and come back to it later when time allows.

- Make photocopies of key sections or articles that you can annotate to highlight key parts and summarize themes.

- Make notes of the important points and key quotations and the ideas that they prompt.

- Give yourself regular short breaks from reading to maintain concentration and focus; do not read when tired.

- Ensure that you understand what you read. If you do not and it is critical to your essay, make sure you clarify things with a lecturer or fellow student as soon as possible.

Some people can scan read – that is, they can quickly look over some text and get a sense of the argument. This is not a requirement for essay preparation, but you should find that with practice and increasing confidence in your subject matter you are able to read and make notes on large volumes of written material with greater speed.

During your programme you will be expected to develop each of the academic skills noted above. Try to keep in mind that the essays and other tasks that form part of your course and assessments will have been designed to help you do just this.

READ ON ...

Earlier in this chapter we discussed the rules or conventions that apply to essay writing. One of these was the formality of the style. The next chapter looks at the importance of spelling, grammar and accuracy in some detail. It also considers what makes for good writing, what the rules are and how to develop your own style.

Your notes

....

....

....

....

....

....

....

....

....

....

CHAPTER 2

The foundation for success

In this chapter we look at the contribution of language to the quality of your finished essay. Of course if you write rubbish it will still be rubbish, however elegantly it is written. But language can make an essay that is good in content shine. Attention to language removes errors that can get you marked down, ensures clarity and can help where original and appropriate description makes what you have to say stand out. It is worth getting it right.

Let us begin by making an overall comment in a way that illustrates an important lesson.

Using clear language

If you undertake to engender a totality of meaning which corresponds with the cognition of others seeking to intake a communication from the content you display in an essay there is a greater likelihood of results being less than you hope.

You are correct. That is not a good start. If we want to say: if you write well, people will understand and be more likely to mark you accordingly – then we should say just that. It makes a good point with which to start this section. Language and how you use it matter. Exactly how you express things has a direct bearing on how they are received; and that in turn has a direct bearing on how well your essays will read and how they will be marked.

Make no mistake, habit and the ongoing pressure of studies can combine to push students into writing on 'automatic pilot'. Sometimes, if you critique something that you wrote you can clearly see something that is wrong. A sentence does not make sense, a point fails to get across or a description confuses rather than clarifies. Usually the reason that is not that you really thought this was the best sentence or phrase and got it wrong. Rather it was because there was inadequate thought of any sort – or none at all as you rushed.

It is clear language that makes a difference. This is a serious understatement: language can make a very considerable difference. And it can make a difference in many ways, as we intend to show. Think of text you must read. What makes something good or bad, easy to read or hard work? It might help consider the next section here to look at an example and make a list. Certainly matters like using the right words, arrangement of words, grammar and punctuation and a straightforward approach all help.

The dangers

While the cause may lie in 101 details the dangers of poor writing fall into four categories. What you write may be:

1 *Ambiguous, unclear and thus misunderstood:* you may make a good point but it is unclear and unappreciated.

2 *Difficult to read:* something that makes concentration difficult and thus risks the message being diluted as the reader struggles to take it in.

3 *Wrong:* if grammar and syntax are incorrect this may lose you marks (in some subjects more than others) and if they are sufficiently bad it may lead to a lack of clarity.

4 *Wrong and annoying:* there are some linguistic inaccuracies that are not only noted as incorrect, but which produce a 'surely they know that' response that does extra harm (examples of such are flagged as we move on).

TAKE NOTE

An important point to note is that the danger is cumulative. In other words, while one error may do no great damage (unless it prohibits understanding) the effect of several – or many – mounts up, quickly creating a picture of ineffectiveness that can lose you marks.

Before we get to some examples of fine detail, we consider matters overall in terms of three broad intentions. You need to get it write [sic]. Your lecturers want your essays to be understandable, readable and straightforward.

1. Understandable

Once something is in writing any error that causes misunderstanding is made permanent, at least for a while. The necessity for clarity may seem to go without saying, though some, at least, of what one sees of prevailing standards suggests the opposite. The fact that it is all too easy to find everyday examples of wording that is less than clear makes the point. For example, just consider the following everyday howlers:

> A favourite is a sign seen in a hotel. On the inside of bedroom doors it reads, 'In the interests of security bedroom doors must be locked before entering or leaving the room.' A good trick if you can do it.

> For a while there was a notice on London's Paddington station that read, 'Passengers must not leave their baggage unattended at any time or they will be taken away and destroyed'. And, no, this does not mean gallows are hidden below Platform 7.

Both of these are but a single sentence, yet they apparently cause problems. In the first example the sentence was written, printed and fixed to 256 doors and still no one noticed it was nonsense. If one sentence can be problematical then a full essay certainly can. You could doubtless extend such a list of examples.

TAKE NOTE

The point here is clear: even in everyday situations and even when people are (we imagine) being careful it is all too easy for the written word to fail. Such examples were probably the subject of some thought and checking, but not enough. Furthermore these are only a single sentence long; if that presents problems how much more care is necessary in writing a complete essay. Put pen to paper and you step onto dangerous ground.

So, beyond the link to academic study the first requirement of good writing is clarity. A good essay needs thinking about (which is what a systematic approach to writing, which we describe later, allows, indeed prompts) if it is to be clear, and it should never be taken for granted that understanding will be automatically generated by what we write. Some of the factors that help clarity immensely include using the right words and arranging them in an order that makes your meaning clear; and correct structure: the use of paragraphs, headings and sequence.

2. Readable

Readability is difficult to define, but we all know it when we experience it. For instance:

- your writing must flow;

- one point must lead naturally to another;

- the writing must strike the right tone;

- you must inject a little variety;

- above all, there must be a logical – and visible – structure to carry the message along.

As well as a clear beginning, middle and end the technique of 'signposting' – briefly flagging what is to come – helps the reader understand where something is going. So you might use a phrase like, 'In the next section I will deal with X, Y and Z', then take each in turn. It allows your lecturer to read on, content that the direction is sensible. It is difficult to overuse signposting and it can be utilized at several levels within the text, for instance to flag the nature of what is coming, say an example, as well as content.

Two factors that have considerable influence here are good punctuation and correct grammar. We consider examples of both as we continue.

3. Straightforward

In a word (or two) straightforward means simply put: follow the well-known acronym KISS – Keep It Simple, Stupid. The 'KISS' principle means using short words where they are clearer than long; short phrases, sentences and paragraphs albeit amongst longer elements but enough to keep the reader proceeding easily. In the same way that saying 'now' rather than 'at this moment in time' is usually better, everything about your writing must be designed to make your essays straightforward.

The key to keeping writing simple is using:

- *Short words:* why 'elucidate' something when you can 'explain'? Similarly, although 'experiment' and 'test' do have slightly different meanings, in a general sense 'test' may be better; or you could use 'try'.

- *Short phrases:* do not say 'at this moment in time' when you mean 'now', or 'respectfully acknowledge' something, when you can simply say 'thank you for'.

- *Short sentences:* having too many overlong sentences is a frequent characteristic of much poor writing, from essays to business reports. Short ones are good. However, they should be mixed in with longer ones, or reading becomes rather like the action of a machine gun. Many student essays contain sentences that are overlong, often because they mix two rather different points. Break these into two and the overall readability improves.

- *Short paragraphs:* or certainly not too long. Regular and appropriate breaks as your argument builds up do make for easy reading. In fact a mix of paragraphs works best: more of this later.

TAKE NOTE

Examples in the next section can also be related back to these three overall principles. Success here, let us be clear, comes from a number of details and, while this is not intended as a comprehensive guide to writing and grammar, here we highlight a good number of points. Nothing here is intellectually taxing, but you need to note areas and approaches that you want to avoid or deploy and develop the good writing habits that make better writing a reflex.

Detail that makes for good writing

Some of the detail now highlighted makes an individual point while other guidelines affect your whole text; all are important and all can make a difference. This list may well lead you to further investigation and certainly suggests that some checking as you go may be advisable.

ACTION

Any student needing to write essays should have a guide to grammar and writing style to hand (something like Bloomsbury's *Good Word Guide*) and make a point of consulting it when necessary. Doing so only takes a few seconds and the lessons will gradually stick, reducing the number of times you need to check.

Spelling

Make no mistake, accurate spelling matters and we are not all perfect at it. It is worth the time and trouble of checking to get it right. Be careful with the spellchecker facility on your computer: it will not highlight mistakes that involve one word being written instead of another (check/cheque or write/right and similar) and care is also necessary over matters such as proper names. A dictionary is clearly useful as perhaps is a reference book that will enable you to take in common errors and is not too much of a chore to read. A good example of such a book is Bill Bryson's *Troublesome Words* (Penguin).

Never forget that as examinations are normally handwritten, there is no computer spell checker to hand, and any necessary improvement to your spelling ahead of exams will clearly make you better able to submit the quality of work you want.

ACTION

Resolve to develop the habit of spell checking everything you type, even draft documents you may think do not need it. Not only will this make sure that you do not neglect it when it does matter, but also if you have blind spots then repeatedly seeing a word corrected will help you remember its right form. This is important because handwriting an exam essay allows no such electronic check to be made.

Punctuation

This matters too, not just because it should be correct, but because a well-punctuated piece of text is inherently more readable, and less subject to ambiguity, than one that is not: too little is exhausting to read, especially coupled with long sentences. Too much punctuation can seem affected and awkward. Certain rules do matter here, but the simplest guide is probably breathing. We learn to punctuate speech long before we write anything, so in writing all that is really necessary is a conscious inclusion of the pauses. If you are not sure about this just read what you write out loud – if you find it uncomfortable or run out of breath then you need more punctuation. The length of pause and the nature of what is being said indicate the likely solution. In some ways too much is better than not enough. Particular points to note are:

- *The full stop:* this ends a sentence. So if you write sentences that go on for too long (and breathing will tell you), you need more of them.

- *The comma:* this helps define clauses (simply that's part of a sentence) and separate out elements that need to stand out on their own. In such a case, to explain further, a comma is necessary before and after the separated text (as in this sentence).

- *The semicolon:* this introduces a longer break than a comma and is particularly used to highlight a change of nuance or contrast between clauses; just like this.

- *The colon:* provides a slightly longer pause than a semicolon and is used to introduce a list or a quotation. It also makes clear when something is the result of something else or explains it. Thus – punctuation is important: it influences the quality of your writing.

- *Brackets or dashes:* most often these are used to separate something that adds a note of explanation or gives an example (thus keeping it separate from the main text of a sentence).

- *One dash:* this is a longer pause then any so far and is most often used to lead to something that must be given a separate emphasis, rather in the way of a punch line for a joke – boom, boom.

- *The question mark:* is perhaps an obvious one; it replaces a full stop when the sentence poses a question, which may be actual or rhetorical. See?

- *The explanation mark:* an easy one to overuse or use inappropriately. An explanation mark adds emphasis, for instance producing a shout. It can be regarded as a weakness in that it may be used as a substitute for the more powerful, descriptive language that should feature in your essays. Take note!

- *The apostrophe:* this is renowned for its misuse (the phrase the 'greengrocer's apostrophe' has entered the language. It is not 'Orange's 50 pence'). The apostrophe indicates possession as in 'Patrick's computer' or 'students' computers'; the latter positioning of the apostrophe after the letter s for when the plural is involved – more than one student, in this case. Another use is the intentional omission of a letter as in 'let's' meaning 'let us'. Because this is so often misused and its misuse so often commented on, it is very much one to get right.

- *Headings:* a comment about this fits in here because a heading also prompts a pause and indicates a significant change of topic. Headings also affect the look of a page and some documents need to look easy to read and accessible. Note that headings are usually not appropriate for academic essays. In some subjects you may be able to use them, but check first.

Making up the page

Even the densest text is normally broken up into paragraphs, what the dictionary calls a 'section of the text'. The practice in recent years has become to use shorter paragraphs than in the past, and certainly very long ones can seem daunting to read. There is no definitive rule for the structure of paragraphs, but each needs to focus on a discrete issue; when the topic moves on you need to start a new paragraph. If complexity is involved within single paragraphs then they need a beginning, middle and end to keep them well-ordered and clear. The first sentence of a fresh paragraph should make it clear that something new is being said; the middle sentences explain it; and the last links on to the next paragraph and the next part of the essay. As not including overlong paragraphs is being recommended it should perhaps be noted that there is virtually no minimum length for a paragraph, indeed an ultra brief one adds emphasis.

Brevity in this context really does make something stand out. See?

TAKE NOTE

There can be no definitive view of such things (short paragraphs). While it is certainly a valid writing device and can lend emphasis to certain texts and arguments, it should be noted however that some lecturers regard this sort of thing as a step away from an acceptable 'academic style' and either dislike it or forbid it. Such a view makes a good point that certain practices in writing may be useful but must, first and foremost, be compatible with the approved style of your university, your subject and lecturer. The moral is: if in doubt check; you will only need to check such matters once early on.

The overall rule is that if you are in doubt about when to move to a new paragraph then err on the side of more paragraphs rather than fewer. This is an important aspect of writing an essay and more information, for those who want more detail, appears in the next section.

Perfect paragraphing

Some students express concern about paragraphs and specifically how to judge their length. Doing so is important, but it is not complicated and a commonsense approach is all that is necessary. A paragraph is simply a subdivision in a longer written passage. It normally deals with one particular point or theme within the totality of the piece – the essay in this case. Essentially it is an element of punctuation, making a piece easier to read and easier to follow in terms of the flow and the argument. There is no set rule about paragraph length. They can be long or short. Some paragraphs, as has been mentioned, can be very short. Others could be a page or more, though do note that both the shortest and longest are rare and you should take care in their use. What works best is usually a mixture of longer and shorter paragraphs within the middle range. Aim to vary length therefore rather than look for a set formula. For instance this particular paragraph contains over 150 words and that is probably about average for what would most often be used in an essay.

Essentially there are two ways to check that they are not getting too long. First there is the number of words. This gives a crude guide and allows you to check if what you are writing is getting out of hand. The second relates to content. If you clearly go onto a new point then you need a new paragraph. If the point is long and in danger of creating an overlong paragraph then you need to word it in a way that allows a break, even if in some sense the break does not dramatically change the nature of the point being made. Take this piece of text here. Reviewing the nature of paragraphs and how to deal with them is one topic, but doing so in one long paragraph would make too long an unbroken section. So it is split: each paragraph moving on sufficiently to be seen as a 'new topic' in paragraph terms. Doing this makes for an easier read.

Another aspect of the paragraph is also helpful in judging length: its internal structure. The first sentence (just like the one before this) needs to indicate something of what the new paragraph moves onto. Such a sentence can be a general description or it can be more specifically handled. Here are three examples:

1 It can link back to the question – 'However, the way the question is put also suggests ...'.

2 It can recap – 'In the last section ..., now we look at ...'.

3 It can flag what's coming – 'Next we turn to X and Y.'

Similarly there may usefully be a link in the final sentence of a paragraph taking the reader from one point to the next to help keep the logic flowing. When the content of the paragraph has been covered, you add a final linking sentence and move on, starting a new one. If, despite some thought beforehand, you find a paragraph is going beyond your expectations of length, then you need to find a way to break it up, but you must do so in a logical way.

As a final check, here and in practice, just consider the appearance of your text. The boxed paragraph repeats the text from the last four paragraphs. It is not intended that you read all this again. Just look at it: it is represented as one long paragraph. It is all about paragraphs, but it is clearly too long. Even broken up a little by a short, indented numbered list it appears dense and is too long.

SEE THE DIFFERENCE

Some students express concern about paragraphs and specifically how to judge their length. Doing so is important, but it is not complicated and a commonsense approach is all that is necessary. A paragraph is simply a subdivision in a longer written passage. It normally deals with one particular point or theme within the totality of the piece – the essay in this case. Essentially it is an element of punctuation, making a piece easier to read and easier to follow in terms of the flow and the argument. There is no set rule about paragraph length. They can be long or short. Some paragraphs, as has been mentioned, can be very short. Others could be a page or more, though do note that both the shortest and longest are rare and you should take care in their use. What works best is usually a mixture of longer and shorter paragraphs within the middle range. Aim to vary length therefore rather than look for a set formula. For instance this particular paragraph contains over 150 words and that is probably about average for what would most often be used in an essay. Essentially there are two ways to check that they are not getting too long. First there is the number of words. This gives a crude guide and allows you to check if what you are writing is getting out of hand. The second relates to content. If you clearly go onto a new point then you need a new paragraph. If the point is long and in danger of creating an overlong paragraph then you need to word it in a way that allows a break, even if in some sense the break does not dramatically change the nature of the point being made. Take this piece of text here. Reviewing the nature of paragraphs and how to deal with them is one topic, but doing so in one long paragraph would make too long an unbroken section. So it is split: each paragraph moving on sufficiently to be seen as a 'new topic' in paragraph terms. Doing this makes for an easier read. Another aspect of the paragraph is also helpful in judging length: its internal structure. The first sentence (just like the one before this) needs to indicate something of what the new paragraph moves onto. Such a sentence can be a general description or it can be more specifically handled. Here are three examples:

1 It can link back to the question – 'However, the way the question is put also suggests ...'.

2 It can recap – 'In the last section ..., now we look at ...'.

3 It can flag what's coming – 'Next we turn to X and Y.'

Similarly there may usefully be a link in the final sentence of a paragraph taking the reader from one point to the next to help keep the logic flowing. When the content of the paragraph has been covered, you add a final linking sentence and move on, starting a new one. If, despite some thought beforehand, you find a paragraph is going beyond your expectations of length, then you need to find a way to break it up, but you must do so in a logical way.

The splits that were made in the first appearance of these paragraphs render it into logical separate parts, essentially: an introduction, advice about checking length, something about structure, and a further and separate aspect of checking length. The whole piece focuses on the need not to make paragraphs too long, to vary their length and make sure that you preserve your writing as you sectionalize it into paragraphs. Next we turn to more detail within a paragraph.

Within the paragraph

The units within the paragraph are the sentence and the clause. In more complex sentences there may be several clauses and these may be different in form:

- It is clear that a sentence must read well. (This sentence has a noun clause providing a subject for the sentence.)

- The sentence that John wrote did read well. (Here an adjectival clause describes who wrote the sentence.)

- John wrote the sentence as he sat at his desk. (An adverbial clause complements the verb, telling about the circumstances of his writing.)

TAKE NOTE

For the record let us be clear about the terminology here:

An adjectival clause is a dependent clause that modifies a noun (thus, above, it defines the sentence referred to as the one John wrote).

An adverbial clause is simply one where a phrase plays the role of an adverb, ie it modifies a verb as 'quickly' changes and modifies the word 'write' – 'write quickly'.

Such clauses make a sentence more logical and allow less opportunity for ambiguity. The box below provides some more information about clauses.

TAKE NOTE

The technical detail regarding clauses can be summarized thus: a clause is just a group of words and a main clause can stand alone as a sentence. In the sentence: 'He continued working on his essay because of the deadline', the words 'He continued working on his essay' is the main clause and 'because of the deadline' is a subordinate clause that adds further explanation and meaning. Also worth noting is the relative clause, which usually starts with the words 'which', 'that', 'who' and so on. For example: 'My brother, who was at university, continued working on his essay.' The words 'who was at university' form a 'defining' clause: that is it implies that there is only one brother. Written without commas – 'My brother who is at university continued working on his essay' – it implies that there may well be more than one brother (others who are not at university). Precision in this kind of way will always enhance clarity and thus it is worth getting right.

Grammar

Certain things can jar; and you should be particularly careful to avoid things that examiners and lecturers will notice and dislike. To give an immediate example, 'less' and 'fewer' are often confused: one refers to quantity (less), the other (fewer) to numbers. In addition, in correct usage 'less' tends to go with singular nouns (less money), and 'fewer' with plural ones (fewer students). Some mistakes are very obvious; other things you may need to check and get into the habit of either using or not using as appropriate.

Grammar is a huge topic, one that you may feel stands some more elaborate study, and we can only give examples of the kind of thing needed here. We approach this primarily by listing examples in terms of what to avoid. First let us note that some rules are meant to be broken, or more accurately some 'rules' are now archaic. Certainly the main thing is that what you write reads well. As the writer Keith Waterhouse said in *English our English:* 'If, after all this advice, a sentence still reads awkwardly, then what you have there is an awkward sentence. Demolish it and start again.' For example, one example of archaic rules are those that forbid starting a sentence with the words 'and' or 'but'. Maybe years ago this rule was the norm. But it is not so today. And besides it can, provided it is not overused, create writing that does read well. But be careful; some such practice is adopted more slowly in academic circles and we found more than one lecturer who still regarded this as a rule not to break. Perhaps the moral is if in doubt check, or adopt the more formal alternative.

That said, here are some examples of things to take care over:

- *Split infinitives:* the most famous of these comes from the title sequence of *Star Trek* – 'to boldly go' rather than 'to go boldly'. These days split infinitives seem more tolerated, but it is not something to overuse.

- *Adverbs:* Some incorrect use here can throw pedantic tutors into fury. For example, 'hopefully' is often used ungrammatically. Hopefully we will write well. Here it is a self-functioning statement and should be written as 'It is to be hoped that ...' or, 'I hope ...'.

- *Mixed subjects:* sometimes this awkwardness gives the wrong impression. 'Having worked through the night, the essay was finished on time.' It is not the essay that worked late, but rather the writer.

- *It:* the word 'it' can be loosely used in a way that causes problems. A famous example is, 'If the baby does not thrive on raw milk, boil it.' Clearly the word 'it' here refers to the milk not the baby, but this could be better expressed. Another danger is that of distance. Something is referred to, discussed at length perhaps, and then some sentences later a new sentence starts with 'It is ...' but so long after the original thought that it is not clear what is referred to by the word 'it'.

- *Double negatives:* a sentence like, 'I cannot believe that there may not be a problem here' begs the question – is there a problem or not? An area for some care.

- *Incorrect and annoying:* some things, for whatever reason, are both wrong and annoying. A good example of this is the use of the word 'unique'. 'Unique' means unlike anything else and so you must not write 'very unique' or 'rather unique'.

- *Tautology:* (or unnecessary repetition) of which the classic example is people who say 'I, myself personally' and is to be avoided. Do not export overseas, simply export; do not indulge in forward planning, simply plan.

- *Oxymoron:* (word combinations that are contradictory) may sound silly – distinctly foggy – or may have become current good ways of expressing something – deafening silence. Some sentences can cause similar problems of contradiction – 'I never make predictions; and I never will'.

This is necessarily a disparate group of points chosen intentionally to span the range of things that are important and can assist you make your writing score points. The Action box below sets out a sensible approach to making regular improvements.

> **ACTION**
>
> It is useful to take active steps to develop habits about such things as grammar and punctuation. Try to take note of things you discover that you do out of habit which you should not do, so that when you catch yourself doing them it triggers a response and a change before you even start to write. Similarly, if you make a note of things you *do* want to adopt, you will begin to deploy them as a reflex.

Word use

Words should be chosen with care, both to achieve simple accuracy and make the precise point you want; the choice will impact both meaning and tone. Two aspects are important and go beyond a single word.

1. Using the right words

For example:

- Is your work on an essay *continuous* (unbroken or uninterrupted) or *continual* (repeated or recurring)? Unless you never sleep it is likely to be the latter.

- *Scarce* and *rare* do not mean the same thing: scarce is applied to something currently difficult to obtain, rare implies that there never were very many of something.

- Are you *uninterested* in a proposal or *disinterested* in it? The first implies you are apathetic and don't care either way, the latter means you have nothing to gain from it.

- Similarly, *dissatisfied* and *unsatisfied* should not be confused. The first means disappointed and the second needing more of something.

- *Fortuitous* implies something happening accidentally; it does not mean *fortunate*.

- If something is *practical* then it is effective, if something is *practicable* it is merely possible to do, and *pragmatic* is something meant to be effective (rather than proven to be so).

2. Selecting and arranging words to ensure your meaning is clear

For example, saying: 'at this stage, the case is ...' implies that later it will be something else when this might not be intended. And as mentioned above, beware mixed subjects. Saying: 'after working late into the night, the essay will be with you this afternoon' seems to imply (because of the sequence and arrangement of words) that it is the essay that was working late.

Another aspect of using words is the need not to have too many; to be succinct. You want your argument or information to be described clearly. Of course the content of your essays may be anything but simple, but it needs describing without undue wandering before you find the right words. This should be linked to the overall length of an essay. Most often you will receive clear guidance, or clear instruction. If you are asked to write 2,000 words you want those words to express the content well; poor word choice can have you wandering so much that the total essay fails to contain sufficient substance and may take you seriously over the required length.

ACTION

Always respect the word count (extent) that is given to you. It is courteous and efficient to do so and writing 3,000 words rather than 2,000 is more likely to annoy a tutor rather than score you extra marks.

The important thing here is to have the appropriate level of detail. Avoiding unnecessary complexity and jargon while dealing fully with the intricacies of the subject in simple language is a skill to work on.

Do not underestimate the contribution to a successful piece of writing that careful, correct language can make. We will resist digressing at further length about grammar and correct usage; other sources may be useful here. However, we intend these examples to make a valuable and easily overlooked point about the appropriate use of language: think on and write right. Before we move on to the next topic it is worth adding a word about style.

Personal style

Two points are worth making here. First, do not show off and write in a way that seeks to add substance in a way that actually does the reverse. Avoid, for example:

● Unexplained jargon; it can just confuse.

● Making things unnecessarily complex; even choosing a particular word and ignoring a simpler and more appropriate one may dilute your style and give the wrong impression; for instance – eat/consume, say/communicate, show/demonstrate. An essay may be complex, of course, necessarily so; the point here is not to make any particular pieces of text unnecessarily complicated.

- Unnecessary foreign words and phrases.

- Abbreviations, especially those that are or verge on slang (so an invitation not an 'invite').

- Idioms that make sense only to a specific small group (especially one a tutor is unlikely to be in); this applies to age groups and nationalities for instance.

- Words or expressions out of time; words and phrases have a lifecycle and something new, just coming into use, may be misunderstood or fade away very quickly, and something old-fashioned may be misunderstood or be so overused as to have become weak and meaningless.

- 'Tabloid' language in which everything is dramatized and exaggerated: prices soar and shares crash, minor mishaps become nightmares or disasters, and so on.

TAKE NOTE

The inherent formality of an essay (as described in the last chapter) will provide a barrier that helps avoid errors such as those above; concentrate on getting that element right and it will help avoid some potential errors along the way.

And ... a word about humour. Perhaps this should simply be a note to avoid it, but as there could be some exceptions let's say it is something to be approached with great care. Nothing creates a wrong note more quickly than ineffective or inappropriate humour.

Most people have, or develop, a way of writing that includes stylistic things they simply like. Why not indeed? For example, although the rule books now say they are simply alternatives, some people think that to say: First, ... secondly ... and thirdly ... has much more elegance than beginning: Firstly .... The reason matters less than achieving a consistent effect you feel is right.

It would be a duller world if we all did everything the same way and writing is no exception. There is no harm in using some things for no better reason than that you like them. It is likely to add variety to your writing, and make it seem distinctively different from that of other people, which may be useful in itself provided you do not overdo the quirky.

Certainly, and perhaps above all, you should always be happy that what you write sounds right (the point made earlier about reading out loud is germane here). One more thing may cause problems for some – hence the next section.

If your first language is not English

If you are reading this book then probably you speak and read English; indeed you are no doubt studying in English and will have to submit your coursework in it too. But if this is not your first language then it may make for difficulties.

First, do be aware that whilst a tutor who knows you may make some allowances for coursework that is not as well written as it might be, an examiner is highly unlikely to do so for an examination paper. We consulted a number of lecturers about this. Whatever might be done during coursework, when understanding, help and advice is commonly available, the situation with examinations was clear. As one of our informants said, 'in exams the appropriate standard must be hit and there are no concessions made'.

Speaking two or more languages is a wonderful skill, but if your first language is not English it would be surprising if it was as good as your first. Furthermore, while many people manage to communicate well verbally in a second language, most would agree that writing in it is that much more difficult. What is more, unlike speech where no one is remembering every word you say, written material lasts; it is a lasting record of your competence.

Extra learning

For some people this is so important that they must seek out some extra tuition and learn more about the English language and how to write it. Indeed some universities provide just that sort of assistance; if this is so in your case, such help should certainly be taken. For many people in this position some private study (and perhaps more practice too) is worthwhile. The very nature of English makes for some common mistakes. For example, sentences are constructed backwards compared with many European languages (derived from Latin), so we don't say 'sentences backwards are constructed ...'. Beyond practice and study, what can you do?

Giving special attention

Though everything in this chapter is important and useful, there are a number of areas to which it is worth paying special attention if you are in this position. Actively doing so will improve the standard of your written English and may help to develop good habits that mean that you have the reflex to take care or check in a way that improves matters still further. Factors that demand taking care, and where not doing so can highlight any writing inadequacies, include:

- *Spelling:* English spelling can be quirky and seemingly illogical. Work during your course is most often typed and a spell check can be done automatically, but examination essays must be written and no such assistance is then available. So make sure you learn from the spell checking you do and pay special attention to words that are inherent to your course. If you are studying English Literature you do not want the examiner to find you spell 'narrative' in three different ways in the course of one essay.

- *Missing words:* it is easy to miss out a word and not notice as you read your work over.

- *Wrong words:* it is a characteristic of English that there are many words that sound alike yet that are spelt differently; 'there' and 'their' is a common example. There are also words that seem similar yet are not; for example, 'uninterested' means that someone does not care about something, whereas 'disinterested' means their feeling is neutral, they do not care one way or another. It is worth making the effort to get this sort of thing right.

- *Slang:* academic writing needs a degree of formality. Be careful not to let words that are descriptive in conversation get into an essay if they are inappropriate. In a history essay, for instance, don't describe an 18th century figure as being 'cool' about something.

- *Double negative:* this means phrases like, 'I don't have no time' and (with rare exceptions) they should be avoided – they are, to quote one wit, a no-no.

- *And:* over-complex writing and thus overlong sentences have been mentioned and are a sign of poor writing. Checking how many times you use the word 'and' – which allows long sentences to run away from you – is a useful technique.

- *Fragment:* this is what a grammar check on a computer says when your sentence is ungrammatical and, well, not a sentence; it's always worth considering altering anything that flags this warning.

- *Abbreviations:* coursework and essays are not text messages. Avoid abbreviations and explain those you do use thus: 'Something that was in evidence in the organization was the use of information technology (IT)' – such an arrangement allows you to use the abbreviation (IT) further on in the text.

- *Apostrophes:* this has been flagged already and incorrect usage is regarded as a sure sign of poor writing, so make sure you learn the rules.

- *Overusing words:* if your vocabulary is in any way limited you may need to expand it. Reusing one 'favourite' word shows your limitations and is to be avoided.

Take care with your work, try not to rush and, above all, check, check and check it again. If you can, get an English speaker to proofread it for you. If you can arrange this make sure you take careful note of the amendments so you can learn from them. After all this is not just a matter of refining your skills to help you write good essays: it is developing skills that are great for your career too (something we return to on page 125).

ACTION

Good habits are as powerful as bad ones. Almost certainly you are going to have to change your writing habits. Making a shift to new ways is possible and the rewards make the game very much worth the candle: you'll write more quickly and easily and it will ensure your coursework is immediately understood by lecturers. Make your next essay a starting point.

The net effect of all this is positive. To recap: if whatever you write is clear, answers the question well and meets the academic standards and conventions of essay writing described in the previous chapter then it will be well marked, and will ensure you are considered to be a good and diligent student. It is well worth a little effort to get this right.

READ ON ...

However well you write, you cannot write anything until you have the material you want to write about and your sources clear in your mind. This needs not just preparation but research, and it is to researching the content that we turn next.

Your notes

....

....

....

....

....

....

....

CHAPTER 3

Researching the content

In this chapter we explain how best to identify, gather and select the material that you will need for your essay, including through the use of bibliographies. We start by considering the title or question, and how to select one where you have a choice.

Deciding which topic to write on

Before you can begin work on your essay you need to decide what you are writing about. In some cases the essay title (or 'question') will be fixed, and you just have to get on with it, but in many circumstances you will be given a choice of titles from a list. Where you have a choice think carefully before you rush to begin, and in particular try to choose a topic:

- that interests you – you will be spending a considerable amount of time working on it;

- where the material you need can be relatively easily identified and gathered;

- on which you may have done some preliminary research, for a seminar or following a lecture, for example.

Consider too whether there may be occasions when you should select a more difficult option. It may be that choosing a topic you know less well or a kind of question with which you have had less practice will give you an additional learning experience and better prepare you for work to come later in your course and exams. Doing so may not be the quickest way to complete an essay, but it could sometimes be a useful thing to do.

The questions on the list from which you must select will not just have been quickly cobbled together to get the right number of options. Rather, the topics covered and the detailed wording of the questions will have been considered and refined at length by the lecturer or course convenor to ensure they are clear, appropriate to the course, word limit, materials available and so on. Your selection of a question to answer demands a similar level of reflection.

Before you can select a question, you need to understand it, and you may well need to consider several questions in detail before you can select one with which you are happy to proceed. So the next section looks at ways to help you understand the question(s).

Understanding the essay title

Before you begin the actual work, it is essential that you understand the question that you are answering.

First, read the question carefully. This may seem obvious, but it is easy to miss or misinterpret something. Be particularly careful of the small words; for example, a question may ask you to discuss the statement, 'Marketers are only concerned to ensure customer satisfaction.' That is certainly one concern, but is it the only one? The little word 'only' changes the emphasis.

Think carefully about the question and consider any keywords that will help you plan your response. Most essay titles or questions are relatively formulaic. The main types are:

Evaluate	Consider the value of something (or a range of things), exploring its strengths and weaknesses and arriving at a firm conclusion in your assessment.
Compare and contrast	Place two or more things in relative perspective. Highlight similarities and differences, showing why these are significant. (This is often a favourite term in examination questions as it forces you to demonstrate a breadth of knowledge.)

Analyse, examine, explain or discuss	Explore something in depth to show your awareness of different interpretations and your ability to identify and assess key issues.
Consider to what extent	Determine the degree of importance or impact of something upon an outcome or argument.
Review	Describe and then assess the correctness of something.

Think about the questions carefully; do not see what you want to see. Many student essays fail to answer the question accurately because the student has looked at one or two keywords in a title and then written down everything he or she knows about that topic without recognizing the particular angle or argument that is required.

Most students discuss essay questions informally with each other as soon as they are available; make sure that you get involved in this process as hearing what your fellow students are saying about the essays can iron out any misunderstandings at the start of the process.

For each essay title that you are considering think about:

- What is behind the question? What is it the lecturer wants to see in your response?

- Which primary sources (see Chapter 1) you will need to be aware of for each essay.

- Any secondary sources that you are already aware of, perhaps if they have been discussed in a lecture or seminar.

Time taken at this stage is not wasted: it will ensure that all your future work is properly focused. It is very difficult to put several days into planning and researching an essay only to realize that you did not fully understand the title and now do not wish to proceed with it: you will be back at stage one. At the same time you must be careful not to delay getting started on your assignment just because you cannot select the question that you are going to answer.

ACTION

If you are in any doubt about what is required for a particular question that you are considering answering then speak to your lecturers promptly. This may well save you a lot of wasted time and put you in a position to move on and begin work on your essay with confidence. Do think it through first, however; lecturers will respond better to your seeking clarification about your analysis than what they might see as you avoiding the process and looking for an 'easy answer'.

Once you fully understand what is involved in answering the questions on the list, make your selection and then make sure that you stick to it. Make sure that all of your subsequent research and writing is based on that title. Do not be tempted to include irrelevant material. Use parts of the title, keywords in it, and the title in your own words throughout the essay. This will help keep you on track and show your lecturers that this is so.

Gathering material and using bibliographies

As we noted in Chapter 1 an essay is a significant piece of work. You will not meet the requirements in terms of word length and content without significant background research. If you have already had a lecture or seminar on the topic your notes can provide an excellent overview and a way into the subject, but in themselves they will be insufficient to tackle the essay. The material you may need to consult includes:

- books;
- articles in academic journals;
- DVDs;
- videos and CDs;
- slide and photograph collections;
- newspapers (both recent and archived);
- collections of MA, MPhil and PhD theses by the university's postgraduates;
- digital collections, including some websites;
- experimental data and results.

ACADEMIC JOURNALS

An academic journal is a bit like a magazine. It is published regularly and contains scholarly articles (sometimes around a specific theme), book reviews and sometimes other material. The articles are submitted by academics based on their current research and are all peer-reviewed. This means that before they are accepted for publication they are examined anonymously by other academics in the field for intellectual quality and rigour. All academic disciplines have a range of specialist journals attached to them that are usually a mixture of the general and specific.

For example, *Nature* is a famous journal that carries articles on any aspect of science. At the other end of the scale, but still within the group of academic scientific journals, is *Nature*

Nanotechnology, which is obviously a highly specialist area. *Scientific American* is a general journal publishing articles on a wide range of science subjects, whereas there are many journals focusing on one, sometimes tight, subject area. These range from the *Astronomical Journal* to the *Journal of Chemical Physics*. The humanities have their equivalents. These days many such journals are available online and such sites as J-store.com are useful, though your subject will direct you to appropriate sources and you should be guided by your lecturer.

Academics find articles particularly useful because they:

- contain the latest thinking on a subject;
- analyse specific themes or ideas within a wider context;
- provide succinct explorations of much broader topics.

Some material is inappropriate for academic study because it is not sufficiently comprehensive in terms of its depth of analysis and range of conclusions. Although such material may look initially appealing you should not use it in your essay. This includes A level course notes (both your own and published guides), and websites not from clearly identifiable academic or academic-related institutions. This means, for example, that Wikipedia is not suitable, but the website of The National Gallery is. Discrimination and discernment are still needed: for example, material from a section of The National Gallery website for general visitors or school teachers will not have the level of sophistication required for university study.

You will quickly find that your university library has massive volumes of reference material and identifying which of those items that appear to be relevant is critical. Your first port of call is therefore your bibliography.

BIBLIOGRAPHY

A bibliography is a list of books, articles and other academic reference material, including both primary and secondary sources, relevant to a particular topic. You will usually be given one per course or module. Lecturers spend a great deal of time preparing bibliographies, revising them regularly and taking care to ensure a spread of material designed to give you an overview of the various opinions and interpretations of each topic you study.

If you are very lucky each essay question will come with an individual bibliography. If there is no bibliography specifically for each question there may be a section on each topic on the particular course you are following. Lecturers structure bibliographies in different ways, but you should assume that you should read all the items relevant to your essay as a minimum. In all likelihood you will need to consult more widely and the bibliography will be a starting point. As you read each item keep careful notes. One item will lead you to another, and you need to make a note of it when you see it, rather than spend ages hunting for the reference later.

> The bibliography is the most important piece of information you need for each course. It is a signpost to the different sources you will need to study to do well. Make sure you follow its guidance.

One of the good things about the bibliography prepared by your lecturer is that you can be certain that the items listed will be available in the university library (but not that they will be sitting on a shelf waiting for you when you need them of course, hence the need to plan essays well in advance). However, you may find that as you explore a particular topic and follow up further references you need to obtain an item that is not in your institution's library.

In such cases your university library can carry out an inter-library loans search. These often require the consent of your lecturer in the form of a signature on a request slip, but this should not cause any difficulty. In this case the book will be sent to your library from the holding library and you will be notified when it arrives. But this will take time, again highlighting the importance of planning your essay well in advance to flag such requirements.

> **TAKE NOTE**
>
> Those who staff libraries are usually knowledgeable and helpful. They will probably have dealt with similar queries to yours many times in the past, so do ask and get to know who makes for a helpful person to liaise with regularly. Doing so will stand you in good stead throughout your course.

Selecting material

Once you have tracked down the book, article, or whatever you need, you need to identify the relevant information. In some cases this may only be a small amount on a few pages, in others a whole section, or possibly the whole text.

The best way to extract information is to determine exactly what it is that you need. The bibliography may again help you here. If not, start this process by looking closely at the content pages, indices or abstracts (depending on the type of material). Use keywords to identify which pages or parts you need to read closely. Don't get drawn into parts of the author's argument or narrative that are not relevant to your purpose.

Even if you keep to the relevant material initial research into a topic often brings in a vast haul of material and information, which can be daunting. The pleasing sensation of having a great stash of material can easily be off-set by the fear of having to sort through it. This is why it is extremely important always to bear in mind the title of your essay and the kind of material, information and facts you need.

Once you've started this process you can contact your lecturer, explain the direction you are taking, and check that this is appropriate.

ACTION

Be discerning in your selection and use of materials. Stick to the bibliography and you won't go wrong. Avoid material that has no critical analysis or a narrow range of conclusions. If in any doubt contact your lecturers for advice.

Developing your academic skills

As you select the material, bear in mind the academic skills that you are trying to demonstrate, as we discussed in Chapter 1:

1 awareness of the primary sources;

2 reflection on and analysis of the academic debate, or secondary sources;

3 evaluation of the primary and secondary sources to develop your own argument and view.

In Chapter 1 we looked at why these things are important, and what you need to do; now let's think in a bit more detail about how you would go about them:

1. Awareness of the primary sources

At university it is assumed that you will be aware of the primary sources. For instance, you will not be able to write an essay on Charles Dickens' *Bleak House* without reading the novel first. However, your essay needs to be much more than just summarizing the plot or even the themes: you need to analyse the text to draw out its wider meaning. You need to look at *Bleak House* not just as a story, but as a window on 19th century society, its manners, preoccupations and tastes. You need to think of the book, the plot and the themes as basic facts waiting to be analysed and interrogated to reveal their hidden meaning.

Looking at primary sources demands particular care. If you are studying History and look at a letter from Winston Churchill written in 1941 that proclaims everyone in Britain is work-shy and we'll never win the war, you cannot base an essay on this opinion because it is not representative of his views. The only way to know this is to put it in the context of all his correspondence and you will certainly not have time or means to study it all. This means that you will be reliant upon historians who have done the job already and are able to give a proper perspective.

As we noted in Chapter 1 your ability to engage directly with the primary sources depends upon your subject, but regardless of this you will be expected to be familiar with the content.

2. Reflection on and analysis of the academic debate

The academic debate on a topic will help inform your understanding of the primary sources, particularly where you cannot access them directly, but you need to study the academic debate in its own right as well. You may examine the first carefully argued text on your reading list and buy into the interpretation of *Bleak House* that it presents. However, if you then come to the next equally convincing argument which presents a fundamentally different interpretation then you are going to have some hard thinking to do. You will begin to realize that all the secondary sources include the inbuilt value judgements of the academic scholars who wrote them. However carefully argued and convincing their arguments are, they are simply their opinion. Part of their skill is putting the information together in such a way as to make their case so persuasive.

This point is made to demonstrate the need for you to think critically about the material that you read for your essays. You need to be able to:

- identify where fact ends and opinion begins;
- recognize the personal interpretation that each academic is putting on the primary sources;
- consider if there are other ways to look at them.

It also demonstrates the need for you to read widely around the topic. You don't want to discover that you have relied on one interpretation if there are others available.

Don't be the person who relies upon the one piece arguing that the earth's core is made out of custard, as this might be a deliberately set academic trap to test whether you are researching widely enough and are assessing and interpreting with due care and discrimination.

Mastering the techniques to be able to determine the value of the custard theorist demands time and care. There are several techniques that may help you to do this.

Assess the methodology

Methodology is a term referring to the processes used by academics to carry out their research and is applicable to all disciplines – sciences, social sciences and arts and humanities. Assessing the value of the methodology of a piece of academic writing is a very good way to begin to assess the value of its interpretation of the primary sources.

For instance, the value of a scientific article might be dependent upon the number and type of experiments carried out to gain the data and reach certain conclusions. If this is the case, the authors should be trying to prove their points by clear reference to this method. In the humanities, an interpretation of a novel might require constant reference to the novel itself, and other writings and material by the novelist. If such references were missing, you might question whether the examination was rigorous enough.

Assess the references

Academic studies are usually referenced in full, with brief footnotes or endnotes annotating parts of the text (see Chapter 5 for an explanation of footnotes), and full bibliographic details for each reference at the end. An important aspect of an academic's work is the open display of sources, allowing others to check them if they wish and then, if they believe the interpretation is misguided in some way, they can query and challenge it. If you are looking at a work that is missing a reference to a key primary source, or a secondary source that you know is generally accepted, then you may begin to draw some conclusions about the quality of the interpretation and judgement of that scholar.

ACTION

Don't ignore footnotes. Take any book or article and look carefully at the footnotes and sources: they reveal much about both the breadth and depth of the original research. In addition, you might well be able to access the sources listed in the footnotes, check them out and consider whether you agree with the analysis or not.

Read reviews and abstracts

With time often of the essence in writing essays, identifying the interpretations put upon facts can be greatly assisted by the careful reading of abstracts and reviews. Most academic journal articles are accompanied by what is called an 'abstract'. This is a précis of its content and of the overall argument presented and often appears on the opening page of an article. Reading the abstract carefully is not a substitute for reading the entire piece, but it highlights immediately and clearly the interpretations of the author(s) and gives you something to anchor your thoughts on as you progress through the piece.

Book reviews also often provide very good summaries of a work's content and add the second interesting element of revealing the opinions of the reviewer. Thus, a book review should not be taken as a definitive interpretation of a piece, but as one that might open up other questions and areas for you to consider. Such techniques are all about reading for, and identifying, an argument and interpretation that have been laid on top of the bare facts. They help you to establish the agenda academics have put on their fact selection.

Identify the academic consensus

An important part of the process of analysis is determining the extent to which there is agreement over the meaning of facts and the degree to which there is dissent. You may find two types of dissent. In the first, academics may agree generally on the broad outline of something, but disagree on precise details. However, in the second type there is little agreement at all between the academic scholars in a particular area, with many competing interpretations vying for prominence.

Once again, close reading is a good technique, as academics, particularly in the introductory and concluding sections of their pieces, often position their work in relation to others. In this way, you will be able to sketch out whether there are dominant interpretations and how deeply they are divided from minority positions.

3. Developing your own view

As you examine the academic debate on an issue, analyse the interpretations presented and assess their value you will find that your own view begins to develop quite naturally. You will find that there are some scholars whose work is persuasive, generally accepted and convincing. Other pieces may be less so.

The important thing is how to express your views and how to structure your essay to build up a persuasive argument. Remember that your opinion needs to be considered and informed. Your arguments are only credible when they are grounded in fact and show an awareness of competing interpretations. Your argument will only stand up when it arranges the facts logically and convincingly and reveals that it can overcome different assessments and conclusions. Your essay needs to be balanced, showing if there are different interpretations amongst scholars, but it should not avoid coming to a clear conclusion.

It is important to remember that all arguments and interpretations require refinement and are rarely perfectly formed the first time you either think them through or write them down. This is where formal and informal discussion and interaction with others is essential:

- Seminars are ideal forums for discussion and the presentation of arguments. Use them as opportunities to debate interpretations of facts and identify the opinions of your lecturer and fellow students.

- Lectures give you the opportunity to see how your lecturers interpret primary sources and what value they place on different strands of the academic debate.

- Practical classes where a large group of you may be undertaking a similar exercise give you a perfect opportunity to consider the methodology. Why are you all carrying out the same tasks in the same way? What does this show you about the basic material of your studies and who devised this particular way of approaching it?

- Talking to other students about your studies and specific topics within it may sound slightly nerdy, but it really helps. After all, your fellow students on a programme or module should all be enthusiastic about the basic subject material, so comparing thoughts on different topics may well open up other ways of thinking about a subject or refining your own interpretations further.

However you do it, refining your argument before finalizing the essay in which you present it for assessment is really important.

Making notes

Making notes as you read is critical. You may wish to record:

- a summary of the argument or approach;

- any key quotations, facts or dates;

- questions and issues that need further study or discussion with lecturers;

- references you will or may need to list (making sure that you get all the detail your prescribed referencing system uses; see page 68).

Make sure that you always record the precise bibliographic details of your sources; if you don't know where a key quotation that you wish to use has come from, you may spend a considerable amount of time at a later stage tracking this down.

As you read and make your notes, try to think about where the material will fit into your essay. For example, you may use a quotation to illustrate one side of the academic debate, or you may use it to support your own line of argument. Make sure that you gather enough evidence to present a balanced argument. You don't want to have one section of your essay with little or no references at all, and another part thick with references and quotations.

Using essay banks

Some student unions now maintain 'essay banks' into which students submit their essays for the benefit of future generations. There are also commercial essay banks available online. These can be a useful reference when you want more information on the look and feel of a university essay. However, you should be wary of becoming too dependent on any one individual essay. We have referred to the dangers of plagiarism on several occasions and this applies as much to another student's essay as to the work of an academic scholar. Relying too heavily on an existing essay from an essay bank will mean that you do not develop the necessary academic skills through writing your own essay.

READ ON ...

This chapter on researching the content of your essay has made it clear what a significant task this is. Given the volume of material that you are handling it is not possible to just sit down and start writing as soon as your research is complete. The writing of good essays must be carefully planned, and it is to this topic that we turn in the next chapter.

Your notes

....

....

....

....

CHAPTER 4

Preparing and writing

Having addressed the role of the essay, and how to approach a particular question and the necessary research, we now turn to the actual process of getting the words down. Here we advocate a proven and systematic approach that is straightforward and logical and which makes the process easier and quicker to execute. There is an old saying that planning is easy: it is just anticipating the inevitable and then taking the credit for it. As the last chapter demonstrated, planning is vital as a preliminary to good writing; so too is a sound basis for getting it down on paper.

A systematic approach

Even when you have done thorough research and have assembled the material necessary to inform the content, a good essay is unlikely to spill out of you perfectly formed. It needs some thought and will benefit from the adoption of a systematic approach: one that proceeds a step at a time, logically moving through to the desired end result. Such an approach has several benefits; it allows you to:

- Reflect accurately the question to be answered and the material and content you have assembled to assist you to do so.

- Organize your content to advantage so that the structure is sound and your argument will flow logically and persuasively when read.

- Ensure that your content fits the extent; that is the word count required where this is specified.

- Balance thoughts about what you will write with the question of language – how you will write it.

- Work efficiently so that you complete the task in a reasonable amount of time (this being important as you balance all that needs to be done in your course).

- Hit deadlines; something that is important in its own right.

So, to encompass all possibilities and degrees of complexity, the following seven-stage approach sets out a methodology that will cope with any kind of document (it is the way this book began life too). It is recommended only by its practicality. It works. It will make your writing quicker, easier and more impressive. It can instil the right habits and rapidly become something you can work with, utilizing its methods more or less comprehensively depending on the circumstances. The seven stages are:

1 Listing possible content.

2 Sorting to finalize and arrange sequence and relative import of points to be made.

3 Arranging to organize your notes.

4 Reviewing: a chance to make additional changes.

5 Writing: getting the words down.

6 Editing to fine-tune the writing.

7 Proofreading what you've written.

Stage 1: Listing

This consists of ignoring all thoughts about sequence or structure, and simply listing every significant point that it might be desirable or necessary to include (though perhaps bearing in mind the nature and length of the essay and the level of detail involved).

TAKE NOTE

It should be noted up front that, as stated in Chapter 3, a key part of the preparatory process is developing your own argument. Do not attempt to start planning your essay – or listing content points – until you have thought through your own point of view on the topic and are very clear on this. The structure of the essay will be developed to sell your point of view, or argument, and you cannot do this until you have one! If, at the end of your background research, you are still unclear as to where you stand on all the evidence, you will need to have a further period of deliberation and cogitation before you can start planning.

Once you are clear about your argument, however, you can list things. Consider what this means. As any one essay topic would inevitably be relevant to only a few readers, to give us an example let's consider this chapter of this book, something which, by definition, every reader can examine. The initial 'list' might look like Figure 4.1.

This, a process that draws on 'mindmapping', gets all the elements involved down on paper, both the content and a reminder in this case of the style (Action boxes and so on). It may need more than one session to complete it; certainly you will find one thought leading to another as the picture fills out. Rather than set this out as a neat list down the page, it is better to adopt a freestyle approach.

In this way points are noted, almost at random, around a sheet. This allows you to view the totality of your notes in one glance, so if necessary you should use a sheet larger than standard A4 paper. It is also best done on paper not on screen (the next stages make clear why).

Stage 2: Sorting

Next, you can rearrange what you have noted and bring some logic and organization to bear on it. This process may raise some questions as well as answer others, so it is still not giving you the final shape of the essay. This stage is often best (and most quickly) done by annotating the original list. A second colour pen may help now as you begin to put things in order, make logical groupings and connections, as well as allowing yourself to add and subtract points and refine the total picture as you go. Figure 4.2 extends the example from the first stage (you must imagine a second colour).

Stage 3: Arranging

This stage arranges your 'jottings' into a final order of contents, and here you can decide upon the precise sequence and arrangements you will follow for the text itself. For the sake of neatness and to give yourself a clear guideline to follow as you move

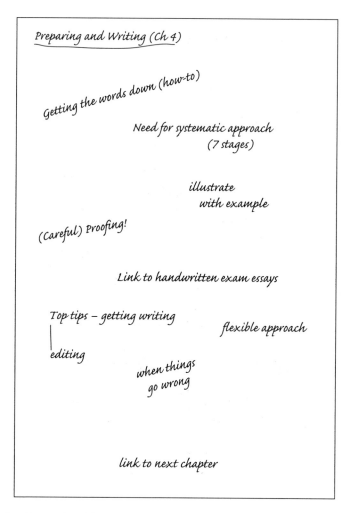

Preparing and Writing (Ch 4)

Getting the words down (how-to)

Need for systematic approach
(7 stages)

illustrate
with example

(Careful) Proofing!

Link to handwritten exam essays

Top tips – getting writing

flexible approach

editing

when things
go wrong

link to next chapter

FIGURE 4.1   Example of 'freestyle' approach to this stage of preparation

on, it is often worth rewriting the sheet you were left with after stage 2 (this is the point at which to transfer your thoughts onto computer screen if you wish).

At this stage you can also form a view and note specifically the emphasis that will be involved. For example, what is most important? Where is most detail necessary? What needs illustrating? (This may involve anything from a graph to an example.) What will take most space?

Not enough material? Usually the reverse is true. And this is the stage at which to prune, if necessary, so that what is included is well chosen, but not inappropriately long. This is true at all levels. Contain the number of points to be made and the amount to be said about each. Of course, you need to write enough to match your purpose, but do not risk submerging it in a plethora of irrelevant detail or subsidiary points that are actually unnecessary digressions. The example continues in the box.

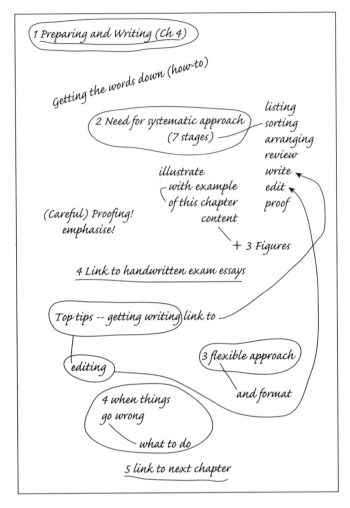

FIGURE 4.2 Sorting: example of this stage of preparation

Preparing and Writing

Introduction

The need for a systematic approach

The seven stages involved (listed)

The seven stages, one by one (note: these might appear here in full)

Examples – Figures

Drafting tips

Editing tips

When things go wrong

Your notes/Read on ...

Action boxes

TAKE NOTE

The amount of detail here can vary to suit you. Something new or complex may need more detail than something with which you are familiar. As a rule of thumb: better too much than too little. (For the record, the details here about this book are abbreviated and of course every chapter needed the same approach, with additional time spent to ensure an appropriate overall flow and logic across the chapters.) You may find it useful to devise a format on which you fill in your final plan: something like the example shown in Table 4.1, though you will doubtless need to personalize this.

TABLE 4.1

The brief/question:
Introduction:
The main content/argument: this can be set out in sections or actually done paragraph by paragraph:
1.
2.
3.
The conclusion:
Notes regarding any necessary references, bibliography, etc:

Stage 4: Reviewing

At this point have a final look over what you now plan to do – review your 'arranged' guideline. It will be quicker and easier to make final amendments now than when you finally print out pages of your draft. It may help to 'sleep on it', carrying out a final review having distanced yourself from what you have done so far. You can easily get so close to something you are working hard at that you cannot see the wood for the trees. One of the things you want to be clear about is the broad picture – if this is right, then the details will slot into place much more easily.

Do not worry if you still want to make amendments at this stage. Add things, delete things, move things about (rewrite your guidelines if necessary) – but make sure that when you move on to write something you do so confident that the outline represents your considered view of the content and will act as a really useful guide.

Let us be clear: when you are writing an essay stages 1 to 4 will take only a fraction of the time of stage 5 – writing. But it is time well spent, as it will reduce the time taken once you start to write. This structure is useful for other documents that you might need to write, and as you develop your own style of this sort of preparation, you will find you can shorten the process a little, and write some simpler documents from the first freehand style list. Where real complexity is involved, of course it will take longer.

With all that has been done so far it is now time to write; and you are now able to do so having separated the decision on *what* to write (at this stage largely done) from *how* to write it. This is significant and makes matters easier and faster.

Stage 5: Writing

What else is there to say? This stage means writing it. This is the bit with the greatest element of chore in it. But it has to be done and the guidelines you have given yourself by preparing carefully will ease and speed the process; so too will bearing in mind what has been said about writing, grammar and so on in Chapter 2. A few practical tips may also help, see box.

TOP TIPS FOR GETTING THE WORDS DOWN

Choose the right moment. We certainly find there are moments when we cannot seem to ... when we are unable ... when it is difficult ... to string two coherent sentences together end to end. There are other times when things flow, when you do not dare stop in case the flow does too, and when you cannot get the words down fast enough to keep up with your thoughts.

Do not struggle. If possible (although deadlines may have an effect here) do not struggle on. If it is really not flowing, leave things. Stop – for a moment, overnight, or while you walk round the block or make a cup of tea. Many people confirm that when the words simply will not flow, a pause helps.

Allow sufficient time. Once you are under way and words are flowing smoothly it may upset and slow the process to leave it. If you feel you need an uninterrupted day, or more, try to organize things that way. It may both save time in the long run and help you produce better text.

Do not stop unnecessarily. For example, you may get stuck over some – maybe important – detail. Say you need to decide on a heading or a phrase, one that must be clear, pithy and fit with the style of the whole thing. You just cannot think of one. Leave it, type some Xs and write on. You can always come back to it (and when you do, who knows, you sometimes think of just what you want in a moment). The danger is that you dither, puzzle over it, waste time, get nowhere and get so bogged down that you lose everything you had in your mind about the overall shape of what you are working on. This is true of words, phrases, sentences and even whole sections. Mark clearly what you need to come back to (so that you don't forget to check it again!)

Other ideas (from the graduates who read this): turn your phone off; work in the library if you have noisy or distracting flatmates; don't be tempted to check your Facebook account.

That said, the job here is to get the whole thing down on paper. It probably will not be perfect, but you should not feel bad about that; very few people can create any document word for word exactly as they want it first time. Practice will get you closer and closer, and things you are familiar with will be easier than something that is new to you or pushes your knowledge or expertise to the limits.

Beware: many essays are handed in at the end of this stage and without the final read through and editing that are required by stage 6. Resist the temptation to skimp in this way and you will always deliver better work.

ACTION

One idea many find useful and which you should consider is to handwrite some of your written work. Why? Because you cannot use a computer in an examination and having to handwrite something when you are used to typing may be a shock to the system, making writing slower and more difficult; content quality can suffer because of this. A few drafts regularly done this way will give you practice.

Stage 6: Editing

The complexities of the material you are using and the arguments you are developing mean that some editing is almost always necessary. There are a number of points here that help make this stage practical but not protracted; the box expands on this with some practical suggestions.

TOP EDITING TIPS

If possible, *leave a draft a while* before re-reading it. You get very close to something and, without a pause, you start to see only what you expect (or hope) is there. It is often much quicker to finish off something in this way than trying to undertake the whole job with one stage back-to-back with the next.

Print out a draft double spaced and/or in a larger typeface to allow plenty of room to annotate it as you review it.

Read things over, out loud is best (though choose where!) You will hear how something sounds, which reflects how it will feel to read. When you do this, you will find that certain things – such as overlong sentences – jump out at you very clearly (you run out of breath).

Get a fellow student to read it. A fresh look often picks out areas you have convinced yourself are fine, for no other reason than you cannot think of a better way of expressing something. Some students habitually do this on a swap basis: because reviewing can be time-consuming, they ask a view of one thing in return for doing the same for someone else. This can work well; better if you do it regularly.

Worry about the detail. Oscar Wilde said: 'I was working on the proof of one of my poems all the morning, and took out a comma. In the afternoon I put it back.' Actually the small details are important. For example, you may create greater impact by breaking a sentence into two, with a short one following a longer one. It makes a more powerful point. See.

Look at the structure. Now all your points are developed in detail does it work effectively? Would moving one particular point or paragraph elsewhere help your line of reasoning develop more logically?

Editing is an important stage. If you need to read it over three times, so be it. Of course, you could go on making changes for ever and finally you have to let something go. But more than one look will be essential.

Stage 7: Proofreading

Once you have a final draft it is critical that you proofread it. A lecturer faced with something clearly inadequately checked tends to think the sloppiness probably applied to the background research too. Make sure you use a spell checker (set to UK English), but remember it is not infallible. One history student, writing about the Battle of Gravelotte, allowed the place name to be replaced throughout an essay with the word 'Travelodge'! So never underestimate the care necessary here. If possible use a grammar checker too.

Spending time on preparation will reduce writing time. Similarly it is usually more time efficient to crack through a draft and then make some changes, rather than labour over trying to make every line perfect as you first write. Like much that is involved here, habit plays a part. What matters is to find an approach for working through all of this that suits you; and prompts a thorough job that produces the end result you want.

ACTION

Using a systematic approach (perhaps having fine-tuned it) really does make writing easier and quicker. It may need a small effort to get into this, but the effort is worthwhile and you will quickly feel the benefit. Tackle your next writing assignment this way and see.

When it all goes wrong

Despite all that has been said, and even with care being taken, there will sometimes be occasions when things do not go according to plan. If, despite careful planning and working hard to your timetable, unforeseen circumstances mean that you cannot complete your essay by the deadline, do not panic. Most universities have arrangements to deal with such cases. They are reserved for serious illness, family difficulties or other exceptional circumstances and you will not get much sympathy if you attempt to use these procedures because of bad planning or lack of work in the allotted time on your part. In such cases:

- Inform your lecturer of the circumstances at the earliest opportunity; letting him or her know a day before, or even after the deadline, of something that has happened a week earlier will not gain you sympathy.

- Continue to work on your essay as your personal circumstances allow so you can complete it as soon as possible and so avoid a knock-on effect on other deadlines and commitments that you may have.

● Comply with the new timetable or deadline given to you or, once again, advise your lecturer at the earliest opportunity if you cannot.

You need to be aware that universities have very rigid timetables for processing the coursework that will contribute to your final degree classification and there will be dates beyond which your lecturers are powerless to go, whatever the circumstances.

Another way in which things might go wrong for you is that you may find yourself completing your essay on time, but receiving a mark for your essay that is much lower than you anticipated, even possibly in the 'fail' category (although careful planning should avoid this). In such circumstances you may be given another chance. You should not rely on this – not least because it means an additional essay to write when you will be busy with existing commitments.

What 'another chance' means will vary by institution. Some universities allow a resubmission on the same essay question, others require a new question to be tackled. Some universities have a strict limit on the number of resubmissions allowed (for example, only one per module). And if you fail an essay it may well be the case that, regardless of the quality of the resubmission, you will receive a maximum mark that equates to the pass mark (which varies by institution but is likely to be around 30 to 40 per cent).

READ ON ...

Next we turn to the detailed structure involved in an essay – the beginning, middle and end – and how to make detailed structural elements contribute to the whole. The next chapter is also where we review how to include references to other works in your essay.

Your notes

....

....

....

....

....

....

....

....

CHAPTER 5

The structure and detail of an essay

Having looked at what an essay is, how you go about the background research and the kind of writing skills you will need to use, we now get down to the nuts and bolts of actually writing the essay, including the structure of an essay and how to include references.

This chapter will cover:

- *making a good start:* how to get off on the right foot with your opening paragraph;
- *the central content:* how to structure the main body of your essay and how to present a clear argument;
- *an appropriate conclusion:* how to ensure a strong finish with your last paragraph and final words.

The introduction: making a good start

The introduction of your essay is critical. Think about a novel. We have all started books that do not interest us at the beginning and didn't read any further. We also know what it is like to be gripped by the first few pages – not only do we want to read on, but we are confident that the book is going to be a good read. An essay is similar. You want to make a good impression right from the start, to give your lecturer confidence that this will be a good essay.

The introduction should tell the reader what to expect from the essay and it is likely to summarize:

- the main areas that will be explored;

- the line of argument that will be followed;

- the academic debate on the topic;

- what conclusions will be drawn.

Beyond this the introduction needs to demonstrate all those skills that we have already discussed. This will ensure that the lecturer reads it and straight away thinks here is a student who knows what he or she is talking about. These skills include:

- familiarity with the primary and secondary sources;

- clear and accurate references;

- accurate grammar and spelling;

- appropriately formal language;

- good organization and structure.

It may well take more than one paragraph: an introduction should not be rigidly identified as the opening paragraph.

Let us consider a hypothetical essay question and compare what would be a good and bad introduction. While there clearly must be a single subject behind the essay question, the lessons drawn from it are wide ranging.

Question: Can any one factor be identified as the cause of the First World War?

GOOD

Historians have argued over the causes of the First World War since the 1920s. Over the decades many complex arguments have been created to explain why Europe fell into war in 1914. In the immediate aftermath of the war the Germans were held responsible for the disaster. Gradually this gave way to the idea of collective responsibility shared among the great powers of Europe. However, in the 1960s the German historian, Fritz Fischer, controversially returned the debate to its origins by once again emphasizing the primacy of Germany in the outbreak of war. Within the immense spectrum of arguments on the cause of the conflict are historians who have singled out one particular factor while others have argued that a range of factors combined to create disaster. This essay will explore the main schools of thought concerning the causes of the war, placing particular emphasis on those who have blamed Germany and those who see it as a disaster either unwittingly or consciously brought about by the great powers.

BAD

This essay is about the causes of the First World War. There is much debate about the causes of the war with some saying that it was down to the navy rivalry and some saying that it was about empires. Others have said it was about domestic issues. Exploring these ideas is a challenging task. In this essay I will try to identify who caused the disaster.

The first introduction is good because it:

- uses clear and precise language throughout;

- shows an awareness of the fact that the arguments and debates on issues and facts change and develop over time;

- moves logically from one point to another;

- tells readers clearly what the essay will do and what they can expect.

The second introduction is weak and exposes the writer because it:

- has no structure – ideas and themes are thrown about without context;

- uses the personal pronoun;

- does not provide sufficient detail, and immediately suggests inadequate research.

Having considered the introduction, let's now move on to look at the main bulk of the essay.

The central content

This part is of course the majority of your essay. It is here where you need to detail your response to the question and develop your argument. A clear and well-thought-out structure is critical and should ensure clarity, making it clear where one point ends and the next begins. Make sure you have a piece of evidence to back up each assertion that you make. It should also make your argument persuasive; you should structure the material in such a way that it reads convincingly, and the argument is built up and strengthened throughout the essay.

Remember that building a persuasive argument is not about only presenting one point of view. Rather you need to show that you are aware of other interpretations, approaches and explanations but point out their weaknesses and shortcomings. In this way you will strengthen your own argument instead of making it look as if you are just brushing 'inconvenient' material under the carpet. Think about the argument as a set of scales where you put evidence on each side. You just need to make sure that the scales are tipped clearly in favour of your own viewpoint.

Break each idea into a separate paragraph, using the first sentence to introduce the idea, and subsequent ones to develop the idea and provide evidence. This will include reference to other material, as well as direct quotation where appropriate. The last sentence in each paragraph should link to the idea contained in the next paragraph; horses closely followed by carts, as it were.

You may find it useful to use headings as you write your essay to group your ideas, material and evidence and so build up your essay as you write sentences to link them. But do remember that, in most cases, these should be removed prior to reviewing your final draft.

At this point we need now to look in detail at what will be a crucial part of your essay (including possibly in the introduction and conclusion) and that is referring to other academic texts. Referencing needs some careful consideration.

Referencing

As discussed in Chapters 1 and 3, one of the things you need to do in your essay is to engage with the academic debate and begin to analyse and evaluate it. You will need to do these things to answer the essay question. You will also need to show how scholars are interpreting the primary sources that relate to your essay. You can do this by:

- relying on the ideas contained in a text;

- paraphrasing a text;

- quoting from a text (this includes diagrams, tables and illustrations as well as words).

Whenever you do one of the above (and you will do them frequently in an essay – or you are doing something wrong) you need to acknowledge (or 'cite') the work you are using. (Some students assume that you only need to cite a work if you quote directly from it; in fact you need to cite it if you use the ideas and arguments contained in it in any way at all.) This may sound onerous and cumbersome, but it is part of the academic convention followed by all scholars to ensure no one is claiming another's work and ideas as their own. There are certain conventions used to refer to other works without interrupting the flow of your text and argument. In the secondary material you read, look at how the author has referenced other material that they depend on for their point of view. The example essays in Chapter 6 of this book will also show you how some students have dealt with referencing.

What this means is that it is critical to keep excellent notes at the research stage of an essay. You really do not want to uncover a brilliant quotation that clinches your argument, but when it comes to writing up your material find you have no idea where it came from. Without this detail, the quotation is useless to you.

TAKE NOTE

How do you actually use the material you wish to cite? Well, you will have to clarify the details with your department or school because there are many different referencing systems in use, and there may be some considerable differences between those in use in the sciences and the humanities. As you read on do bear in mind that some elements of referencing that seem likely to be common – footnotes is a good example – are actually specified as not to be used in some circumstances. Always check; your university will certainly issue specific guidelines.

The following general information is provided to give a broad overview and is followed by some details about one of the systems commonly found: Harvard.

When referencing material within the text of your essay it is sufficient to include just the author and year (for example 'the argument developed by Jones (1994)' or, 'this theory demonstrates (Jones, 1994)') so as not to break the flow of your text. A footnote or endnote is then used to give further details. (Footnotes appear at the foot of the page of the relevant reference, and endnotes appear at the end of the entire essay.)

It is usual to give the bibliographic details (see below) in full on the first footnote, and then subsequently use an abbreviation. Make sure that you use your word-processing program to insert the footnotes or endnotes for you and do not try to do this manually, or you will need to renumber everything if you move text around, or add more detail to certain sections at a later stage.

In addition to any footnote or endnote (where allowed), you should have a bibliography at the end of your essay. For each item consulted, even when you have not used it in your essay, you should include:

The author's name

The full title (in italics or underlined for a book, in single quotation marks for a
  journal article)

Year of publication

Journal name (in italics or underlined) and issue number (if applicable)

Name and location of publisher

Page numbers

Webpage address (if applicable)

Any other information that is needed to allow someone else to find the material.

For example: Forsyth, P., *Disaster-proof Your Career*, Kogan Page, London, 2010,
  p.123

Make sure that you are consistent in how you present references. The essay classification descriptors in Table 1.1 (page 14) make it clear how important accurate referencing is to getting good marks. Fortunately this is one part of the process where you do not have to do more than what is prescribed – it is just a case of learning the system and then sticking rigorously to it.

Next we look at the Harvard system. If you will not use this then the details do not matter though it is worth noting what detail is specified by such a system and resolving to make your own referencing (whatever system it must use) spot on.

TAKE NOTE

Whatever system of referencing may be used on your course, you should check it out and follow it slavishly.

The Harvard system is typical in its detailed instructions. To give a clear picture of this, listed below are the areas on which Harvard lays down rules, together with the individual topics on which detailed instructions are given.

1. Citing references in text

Author's name cited in text

Author's name not cited directly in text

More than one author cited in the text

More than one author not cited directly in the text

Two, three or four authors for the same work

More than four authors for a work

Several works by one author in different years

Several works by one author in the one year

Chapter authors in edited works

Corporate authors

No author

No date

Page numbers

Quoting portions of published text

Secondary sources

Tables and diagrams

Websites

2. Compiling the reference list and bibliography

Books with one author

Books with two, three or four authors

Books with more than four authors

Books which are edited

Chapters of edited books

Multiple works by the same author

Books which have been translated

E-books

Journal articles

Journal articles available from a database

Magazine or journal articles available on the internet

Journal abstracts from a database

Newspaper articles

Online newspaper articles

3. Other types of documents

Acts of Parliament

Statutory instruments

Official publications such as Command Papers

Law reports

Annual reports

Archive material

British Standards and International Standards

Patents

Conference reports

Conference papers

Dissertations

DVD, video and film

Broadcasts

EU documents

Course material

Maps

Quotations from written plays

Pictures, images and photographs

Interviews

Press releases

4. Electronic sources

Websites

Publications available from websites

Electronic images

E-mail correspondence and discussion lists

Blogs

Mailing lists

Podcast or archived television programmes

YouTube video

5. Unpublished works

Unpublished works

Informal or in-house publications

Personal communications

As you can see this is designed to cover how absolutely everything that might need referencing is to be dealt with; exactly how it is to be done is also specified. The inclusion of 'electronic' sources is one that will predictably change fast and makes it clear that such systems are a live entity. Some areas have only a couple of guidelines to follow. For instance, just citing an author's name here demands that i) the date of publication and ii) the relevant page number are included. On other topics there is the best part of a page of instructions and details to be followed. Some need you to get clarification of their exact meaning before you get into any other detail; for example 'Unpublished works' primarily refers to works scheduled to be but not yet published.

No doubt your course will have all the detail you need about whatever system you need to use; the discussion on the Harvard system is more than enough to show that this is something to take very seriously, to note carefully and follow accurately. There are many accessible guides (though you need to check which system you should use), for example, one about the Harvard system is shown on the web from Anglian Ruskin University: www.libweb.anglia.ac.uk/referencing/harvard.htm.

How to present a direct quotation

If you quote directly from the source the relevant part should be put in quotation marks: 'passing off someone else's work as your own, is a major offence' (Connelly and Forsyth, 2011, p. 11). If it is a very long piece, put it in a separate, indented, paragraph (without quotation marks), like this:

> Plagiarism, or passing off someone else's work as your own, is a major offence (and may also involve breach of copyright and copyright law). It includes quoting or paraphrasing another person's work without acknowledgement, and using ideas or arguments developed by another without acknowledgement.
>
> Plagiarism is likely to lead to you receiving a zero for the particular essay involved and, if you persist, it could even mean that you are not allowed to continue your course. Lecturers are used to identifying plagiarism in student coursework, however cleverly it is disguised. Many universities require electronic copies of essays to be submitted so that they can be subjected to plagiarism detection software.
>
> You will be caught. Don't even think about it!
>
> (Connelly and Forsyth, 2011, p. 11)

A final point to help keep you organized – a reference worksheet.

Reference worksheet

For many students, and in many subjects, there may be a good deal of material that will be read, quoted and used in evidence of an argument. You may have material in a number of different forms: pages marked in books you own, photocopies of articles from a library and printouts from the internet. Because all this needs to be organized and noted, having a list you can look over at a glance could be useful – a worksheet is shown in Table 5.1. Remember this is just an example: the precise order and headings must conform to the referencing system that your course demands you use. Give yourself sufficient space; it may be useful to originate such a format on something larger than A4.

The headings are mostly self-explanatory, but to be completely clear note that the first heading is intended to accommodate your own description of the item and the last one, 'Link to evidence', should note something about why you have identified the item and how you plan to use it.

Such a list may finally be culled a little: you might start by including everything that could be useful then highlighting all those items you decide to quote and use that to type the list into your essay in the right format. Be especially careful here to spell accurately: the names and details of references are typical of those where accuracy is not helped by spellchecking.

Having looked at the central part of your essay, let's now move on to consider the conclusion.

TABLE 5.1

	Item Description	Title of Publication	Publisher	Author	Page Number	Chapter Title/ Number	Year of Publication	Place of Publication	Link to Evidence
1									
2									
3									
4									
5									
6									
7									

An appropriate conclusion

The conclusion is the last opportunity for you to show your lecturers that you are a serious student writing an engaging and thoughtful essay. Of course a good conclusion will never make them think this about you if it is following a load of rubbish, but as you have expended considerable time, energy and intellect on the essay up to this point do not let yourself down by a weak conclusion. Sadly, this often happens either because students are running out of steam by this point, or just don't know how to write a good conclusion. The conclusion should be planned in detail in the same way as the rest of the essay.

Your conclusion should not introduce any new ideas or arguments that are not already covered in your essay. Rather it should:

- refer back to the title, and make your own line of argument on the topic completely clear;

- summarize the evidence for this point of view;

- make it clear why this is significant or important (that is, you should set the essay within its broader context);

- show awareness of your position in relation to the academic consensus.

You should also be using the conclusion to demonstrate all those other general academic skills that you will have been using throughout the essay, and that we listed in the section on the introduction.

Your conclusion, as with the introduction, need not be limited to one paragraph, however you must remember that at this point you should be succinctly summarizing your argument and not going through it all over again.

Let's turn back to our hypothetical essay question and compare what would be a good and bad conclusion for this. The title was, 'Can any one factor be identified as the cause of the First World War?'

GOOD

This essay has covered all of the main schools of thought concerning the causes of the Great War. It has been shown that historical interpretations have changed considerably over time. Although the primacy of German guilt has been a constant thread in the arguments, it has been demonstrated that most leading historians in the field now see the causes of the war as immensely complex and overlapping, and that Europe slithered into war in 1914 not by design but by accident. Some would argue that this accident came about only because of earlier deliberately calculated aggressive posturing. This piece has argued that the 'war by accident' approach is the most convincing by carefully comparing and contrasting the strengths and weaknesses of the varying opinions on an issue which is unlikely ever to reach a final, definitive conclusion.

BAD

Many things caused the First World War, and although others can be considered guilty Germany was probably mostly to blame. There are different views on the war with some saying that one nation was the cause and others saying that lots of factors were. The war was about many things and the nations fought for different reasons. The war proved tragic and futile. Finding the real cause is hard as there are so many views, but Germany seems responsible.

The first conclusion is good because it:

- reminds the reader clearly and succinctly what has been covered in the essay;

- demonstrates the complexity of analysis and breadth of research carried out;

- shows awareness of alternative views, but comes to a firm conclusion through a rational and rigorous process.

The other conclusion is weak because:

- there is no definite conclusion and no sense of argument developed;

- it uses emotive language in an inappropriate judgement for an academic essay (and the statement is not relevant to the question set);

- the references to secondary literature are unclear and vague.

And that's all there is to it! Of course, an essay is a significant piece of work, as we make clear throughout this book. However, it is a manageable one, and even a rewarding one. Looking at your essay in these separate parts, taking each idea and paragraph at a time will make it achievable, and something that with time and practice you will get quicker and more confident at.

It is all very well considering these matters as you read this book, and writing coursework essays gives you time to think about it all (provided you are organized!) but writing essays in examinations is another matter; one worth a few words.

TABLE 5.2

Coursework	Examinations
Answers a specific question in great detail	Synthesizes main themes, with a much wider sweep, in a shorter length piece
Rounded, discursive manuscripts	Cuts to the heart of the question as quickly as possible
Follows all academic conventions	No need for full references or bibliographies
Researched and written over a long period	Instant responses based on sound revision and understanding developed through course
Polished and well-crafted throughout	Minor grammatical and spelling errors likely to be forgiven

Writing essays in examinations

Although what we have said in this book applies equally to essays written as coursework and in examinations there are clear distinctions between the two; see Table 5.2. Most obviously the timeframe is different and consequently in an examination you will not be able to do the same detailed and specific background research before answering a question.

Lecturers understand this; indeed the examinations are designed to test a different range of skills, primarily your ability to contextualize information and arguments. It is important to keep this aim in mind as you revise, as you should not be looking to reproduce coursework material in an exam.

The questions that you face will therefore be adapted accordingly (so you are highly unlikely to get an exact question in an exam that you have already written a coursework essay on). Consider the examples in Table 5.3 of real essay questions from a course on the History of London 1750–1900 at the University of Kent, which clearly illustrate the differences, with examination questions being ones that are broader in scope and which can be pitched into, indeed must be, immediately (though a proportion of examination time must be sensibly spent forming a clear plan of how to answer).

The impact of handwriting

Another big difference about writing essays in exams is that you will have to handwrite them rather than use a PC. This can make a considerable and surprising difference, even to the way your mind works. As we handwrite at length so little these days, it will make your hand ache! Although you will want to word-process your submitted

TABLE 5.3

Coursework essay questions	Examination essay questions
Was the fear of crime in London worse than its reality?	What themes dominate the history of London in the period 1750–1900?
Was London culture dominated by middle-class taste during this period?	Did London become a safer city during the period 1750–1900?
To what extent did religion permeate every aspect of life in London?	What was the dominant image of London during the period 1750–1900?
What do the primary sources tell us about the lives of Londoners in this period?	To what extent did the Thames dominate the nature of London's economy?
Did mass consumerism alter greatly the nature of London's economy?	How important was London in setting the fashions in terms of domestic architecture and interior design in this period?
What efforts were made to improve the condition of London's poor during this period?	Why was solving the problem of local government for London so difficult?
How did artists and writers interpret London during the nineteenth century?	

coursework, you should think about other opportunities for handwriting, such as note-taking. You need to be used to writing at length, at speed while maintaining legibility, and note-taking provides the perfect opportunity for this.

PCs IN EXAMINATIONS?

There were reports in the newspapers about this topic just as this book was being completed. Evidently Edinburgh University is seriously considering allowing certain examination work to be written on computers. This is seen as avoiding the 'dual strain' of taking the exam and the psychological brain-twisting of writing when you are used to typing. Dia Hounsell, Professor of Higher Education, was reported as saying 'ten years from now, I'm not sure there will be any handwritten entries in certain subjects'. So, the difficulty is recognized, but who knows when and to what extent any change will come in. The advice here remains firm: be sure you have some practice in handwriting essays and that when you must do so it does not dilute the quality of what you produce.

Other differences in examinations include:

- Writing by hand means no built-in spellchecker. Making sure you know how to spell the key terms, and careful proofreading will be critical.

- Also, not using a PC means being unable to move text around after it is written. This makes thinking about and writing an essay plan before you attempt to answer the question very important. (If you do need to add a section write 'see A below' and then under a heading 'A' write the additional text. Don't just use a star or you'll find it hard to add multiple additions if this is necessary.)

- Working within a short time limit. Whilst coursework has a deadline it is not like the short duration of an examination. You need to plan how long you can afford to spend on each answer and stick to it.

TOP TIPS FOR WRITING ESSAYS IN EXAMINATIONS

- If you have a choice of which essay questions to answer, don't rush to select them. A little longer spent at this stage, thinking about the structure and broad content required, will ensure you make the right selection and don't get halfway through an essay only to discover you don't have quite the right material at your fingertips. In particular be wary of a question that sounds like something you have revised but has a different angle; don't go off down the wrong track.

- If you feel you could tackle more essays than the number required, then think carefully about which ones will allow you to best show the knowledge and views that you have. If an essay question is in more than one part, make sure that you can answer each part; don't be drawn in by a question of which you can answer only one aspect.

- Decide how long you will spend on each essay, and stick to it. Don't forget to check the clock every now and again. Remember to spend time according to the allocation of marks. If you run out of time on one of the essays, take two or three minutes only to jot down the rest of what you would have written in a list of points. Leave a suitable space before moving onto the next one. If you have time at the end you can return to the space you have left and complete your essay in more detail. Always remember to write your list of points before you move onto the next question, while the first topic is still foremost in your mind.

- Make sure that you tackle each essay individually. You may wish to note down initial ideas for each one, but once you have started writing focus on that particular essay, and do so without distraction.

- Plan and structure your essay before you start to write. It is not like using a computer where you can write the text in any order and go back to add large sections of text at a later stage. Time taken planning is time well spent. Consider the number of scripts your examiners will have to mark. Make it easy for them to give you high marks by structuring your essay well, so that the key points stand out. Don't forget that even in an examination you still need a clear introduction, middle and conclusion.

- Once you have finished, take time to re-read your essays (you will need to allow for this in allocating time). You will be writing under pressure and at speed, and may need to tweak a few sentences to ensure their clarity. However brilliant the concept you are trying to express, you will not gain any marks if your lecturer cannot understand what you mean. You must ensure also that your responses are legible, and appropriately laid out for formulae, mathematical symbols and the like.

- It is unlikely that you will be able to leave the examination hall before the end of the exam. If you finish significantly early check if you have completed the paper correctly and written the right number of essays. If you do have some time, don't waste it: use it to check your work again. Correcting spelling and grammar will improve clarity; any aspect of your work you find to amend positively may usefully improve it further.

The focus here has been on *essays* and we have not meant to use the word imprecisely: as has been said, different styles of essay are called for depending on the subject and also on the way a question is posed (whether you are asked to 'discuss' or 'compare' for instance). Before moving on to examine some examples and how you can learn from your own past work, there is another kind of paper that we should define and set apart from the essay: a dissertation. This may be of interest to you now or later; if not you could jump ahead to the next chapter.

The purpose and form of a dissertation

A dissertation is a longer piece of written work than an essay, and may be a compulsory or optional part of your undergraduate degree programme. Much of the general advice in these pages is as relevant to writing a dissertation as to essays: certainly basic issues like writing style, language and grammar contribute to its success; but dissertations are a very particular form. For a start they are much longer than an essay, usually around 10,000 words. Let's make their purpose clear at the outset.

Defining the dissertation

There are five key aspects to a dissertation:

1 Responds to a core question or proposition (sometimes called the 'thesis') and presents a response in a structured, clear line of thought which is best thought of as the 'argument'. The question will be a much broader subject than for an essay question, and may simply be a topic that you explore in some detail.

2 Is of some length. It will contain much more detail than an essay, both in terms of its examination of the question and of evidence reviewed to support the argument it makes. In terms of structure this means that it is normally divided into chapters.

3 Provides evidence of a student's abilities in a rather different way from an essay. This is because the student must select the topic (albeit this can be discussed with a tutor) and necessarily engage in far more independent study, sourcing and assessing the information needed in all its forms, than is necessary to write an essay.

4 Must include explanation about how and why the work has been done in a particular way. In other words it must describe how evidence has been located, analysed and put to work in support of the argument presented. In some subjects the investigative process must follow a prescribed methodology (and this needs checking).

5 Can also mean (in certain subjects) analysing quantitative information. Again there may be a particular methodology to follow and this may include the precise way in which computer programs are used to 'crunch' the data.

All this begins to set the dissertation apart from the essay. Given the length, the other factor is the structure necessary for it. Of course, different subjects and topics will vary in this way somewhat and if you have to write a dissertation you must check the form in your field first and follow it slavishly (again, guidance is usually available from your tutor). That said, the following provides a reasonably general example of structure and certainly shows more about the essential nature of a dissertation and how writing it is very different from writing an essay.

TAKE NOTE

Before we describe the structure it is worth commenting on the presentation of the document. Right from the title page this differs from an essay and it is usual to include some element of graphics. This can include differing typefaces, colour and pictures (everything from photographs and drawings to graphs and diagrams). This is fine: it needs to look good, but it should not be overdone – remember that no amount of window-dressing will make up for a lack of good content. In part, the decision here links to subject and topic, and some demand more of this than others. Be careful about purely 'cosmetic' dressing-up and ensure that the overall effect is always appropriate and professional. If being clever and being clear are ever in competition, clarity must win every time. Sometimes uncertainty about writing the document produces displacement activity: some students spend time on the graphics and presentation not because it is necessary, but because it puts off getting down to writing!

There are seven elements to bear in mind, shown here in sequence. A dissertation will have:

1 *A title page:* this needs to display the title, the author's name (that's you) and also any 'technical' description of what it is and why it is being done – a link to the project, the course and so on.

2 *An abstract:* this is a description that puts what it is 'in a nutshell'. It should be a thorough encapsulation of what the dissertation is and does, and not keep key factors as a surprise within the text. It should rarely be more than a single paragraph and limit the description of the content to:

   – the core question (problem) being addressed;

   – the solution set out;

   – the conclusion of your argument.

3 *An introduction:* you must start by making clear what the question is that you go on to answer. Remember you are not asked to be comprehensive: you can spell out both what you will do and what you regard as beyond your brief. Nor are you necessarily being original or claiming great import for what you do, though you must explain why you believe the question is interesting. The introduction should introduce both the content and the form, so explain the structure you have used and set out the order in which you will deal with matters.

4 *A discussion section:* this is the meat of the matter, where you explore the question and set out a logical, step-by-step argument that, by its end, must explain the conclusion you draw (element number 5). As this is where the

majority of the text will be it should be clearly split into sections; indeed you may need to think about more than just headings, each section may need its own introduction and the sequence described as it begins. One point to note: footnotes may not be expected to be used in great quantity, all necessary points being made en route within the text, but this does vary and, like so much else, you must be sure you know the form that applies to you.

5 *A conclusion:* this is of paramount importance. While not suggesting that other parts of the document should not be clear, it must be *crystal clear* what conclusions are being drawn. The logic of evidence, reasoning and how this informs your conclusions must be spelt out (note that if there are any loose ends, they should be acknowledged and explained – you do not want them to be taken as unthinking omissions).

6 *Acknowledgements:* most such projects demand that you receive some assistance (indeed some would say that without some you may not be doing as good a job as possible). Here is the place to mention library and teaching staff and maybe others who have been instrumental in getting you to the finishing post. This normally makes up a brief section of the whole dissertation, but is important to get it right.

7 *A bibliography and references:* this is an important section, not least to acknowledge your sources and make it clear that no plagiarism has been involved. Referencing is dealt with in detail elsewhere (see page 68) and bibliographies are touched on too (page 44). Exactly how this is done is important and you should follow the letter of the law of whatever referencing system you are expected to use.

The approach described here is common; indeed it will probably fit most circum-stances. The nature of any dissertation goes beyond that of an essay, but the thinking and basic principles that are used in essay writing all apply. Other matters discussed here apply too: time for preparation, careful drafting and checking – care with all is common to both tasks.

On some occasions a dissertation is the most important document that a student will create during his or her course. Making it as good as possible is crucial.

Because you are working independently on your dissertation it is even more important to be disciplined over time management. You must draw up a timetable (and stick to it) to keep you on track. Dissertations left till the last minute are even more problematic than essays; because they are such a significant piece of work the mark you receive is likely to be more heavily weighted in your final degree outcome.

Dissertations that have had insufficient time spent on them are easy to spot. Very often they are significantly short of the word count, and do not explore the topic with the degree of breadth and depth required.

Most lecturers will make time available to students working on dissertations. Make sure you use this time. Don't think that you don't need to see them and not go, because you may well find you do need their help at a later time when they are not available. In particular make sure that you are absolutely clear what you are working on, and that your lecturer agrees that it is an appropriate topic for a dissertation. If you need to twist his or her arm then it is not likely to be a straightforward piece of work for you. You need a topic that you are going to be able to explore in the right degree of academic breadth and depth; a subject that interests you isn't enough to make a good dissertation topic.

READ ON ...

So far we have looked at what an essay is, how to research it and how to write a good one. In the next chapter you will find some actual student essays, reproduced verbatim. You will be able to see how they have interpreted their question, structured their answer, used references and so on. You will also be able to see the lecturer's comments on their essays. You can study these to help improve your own essay-writing technique.

Your notes

....

....

....

....

....

....

....

....

....

....

....

....

....

CHAPTER 6

Example essays and the art of learning from experience

In this chapter we examine examples of essays. Looking at the written word, analysing it and learning from the critique such a review provides (whether you or a tutor lead that process) is a valuable part of refining your own essay-writing technique. This in turn will help you to obtain good feedback and grades. You can refine what you do by looking at what others do and do well.

The following examples speak for themselves. You can see and read what was written. You can see how each was commented on and how it was marked. You can see how things help make something good and how other things make something poor, or at least dilute its effectiveness – often unnecessarily. By observing good examples and the comments that they prompt you can learn something about what to do and what not to do.

A caution: the intention here is to lead you into a useful habit of observation and analysis. It is not suggested that you do best by copying the work of others slavishly in every detail. Your own style, as we have been at pains to point out, can and should help you. And the very real dangers of plagiarism have been spelt out firmly (see page 11).

What your lecturer wants

As has been said there are general overall criteria that define the academic essay. Alongside that, each subject will impose additional disciplines on those studying it and so too will an individual lecturer. We are not suggesting that lecturers will play fast and loose with the rules, only that they may feel strongly about certain things being done a particular way or deviations they will not accept.

TAKE NOTE

Listen especially carefully when you get your first essay-writing assignment. Ask questions if you are uncertain of anything and check if anything appears not to have been mentioned that you think might be important. If possible it may be useful to get the lecturer to give an overview of his or her perspective on what constitutes a good essay (see example below) as such a description may cast further light on how you will need to do things.

One of the people who kindly organized one of the example essays that follow is Jonathan Smith, Senior Lecturer at the Ashcroft International Business School at Anglia Ruskin University, and he also kindly volunteered the following personal overview. Of course this is conditioned by his work and the topic he teaches, but his example does show that such statements are potentially valuable.

In answer to the question, what constitutes a good essay, he wrote:

What follows are my personal opinions to this question, and these are not necessarily linked to my university's policy or their view.

I think the answer to this question depends on the level of the qualification being worked towards. The requirements will be different at Foundation degree, degree, Master's and PhD levels. The guide provided for the module and assessment marking criteria should clearly outline what the requirements are for a good essay and what students have to do to achieve particular marks.

As I work mainly at Postgraduate level I would like to focus my answer on what I believe constitutes a good essay. Again the requirements for particular modules will be detailed quite specifically with the assessment criteria for that module.

Before starting we must also clarify what we mean by 'good' and what we mean by 'essay'. Here I interpret 'good' as an essay that is likely to achieve a high mark – distinction level – which achieves a mark of more than 70 per cent. I am interpreting 'essay' as something written by an individual student which specifically addresses the assignment question that has been set.

The first priority is of course to answer the question that has been asked. This sounds obvious but it is surprising how many students don't do this. It's not always as easy as it sounds either because there can be many different interpretations of questions or because wording can sometimes be confusing and have different interpretations in different cultures. If you are not sure what the question is asking it's always useful to clarify with the assessor if you can. It is also useful to read over the question several times and discuss with friends and family if you can before starting to write your answer.

One of the key differentiating factors at Postgraduate level is that the answer includes an appropriate depth of critical analysis. This means it is not just writing down what other authors have said, or describing models and theories. It also means going beyond just applying these theories in a particular context. A good essay will really question and challenge what people say, current thinking and ideas.

The essay will need to be laid out clearly so there is a clear structure that is easy to follow. It must also be easy to read and follow your argument. I think sometimes that students try to use big and complex words to try and impress the assessor. Of course when you are exploring complex areas sometimes the wording by necessity has also to be complex, but for me personally I would much prefer the wording to be kept simple whenever possible. Also think about your reader. What level of knowledge are they likely to have on the subject, what are they going to want to know specifically?

A final point is to try to keep the essay succinct. There are usually word limits placed on answers and these are often a maximum so don't go over this. It's easy to use five words when actually one will do, and to say the same things a number of times in different ways.

Perhaps that note provides a perfect place to end this outline of my views.

TAKE NOTE

It is perhaps worth pointing out that this statement says that many people misinterpret the question set for their essay – and the implication is that this is wholly unnecessary. This makes the point that clarifying anything unclear upfront is always essential.

A checklist

It is useful to have a checklist that you run through before you hand in an essay. However careful you have been, it can act as a useful backstop and give you a chance to make any necessary last minute alterations. It is good advice to use something of this nature every time.

You will not be able to read an essay relating to a subject you are not familiar with and judge some things – like whether the references are well chosen and set out. But all of the questions in the checklist are relevant for your own work and most of them are worth bearing in mind as you read through the examples shown here. You can see what the individual lecturers thought about our examples and you can rate them to some degree yourself as well.

ESSAY CHECKLIST

1 Is it the right length?

2 Does it answer the question set in exactly the way prescribed?

3 Has it considered all the relevant primary and secondary sources?

4 Are the references and bibliography complete?

5 Does it provide evidence to support its argument?

6 Does it come to a definite conclusion?

7 Is the balance of material right? (Make sure it doesn't focus primarily on one area of personal interest, or miss additional material that is available; ensure that the essay is balanced.)

8 Has spelling in the essay been accurately checked or are there any errors? (In particular, make sure key terms and people's names are spelt correctly.)

9 Has proofreading been done to catch errors other than incorrect spelling?

10 Does it read satisfactorily? That is, does it flow, is it easy to read, is any description used appropriate and does it give the right impression, and – above all – is everything clear and unambiguous?

Note: it can also be useful to check whether any comments, criticisms or suggestions made about your previous work have been taken on board and acted upon. (A further checklist about this appears on page 119.)

The nature of the examples

The range of essays students must write in different courses is huge. It is simply not possible to have an example of everything and we have therefore selected carefully to provide examples that we believe will make this section widely useful. The essays were all written over a period of a few years prior to this book being written. The examples that follow are:

- *Real:* actual essays and the real comments and marks they prompted seem to be likely to be of most use – indeed swapping essays with fellow students is a proven and useful tactic and one we would certainly recommend.

- *Complete:* many books contain extracts from essays (real or contrived) but what is most useful is seeing the whole shape of something in order to critique how well it works.

- *Understandable:* and thus not relating to too specialized a subject. We have therefore avoided technical topics (there is nothing here about quantum physics for instance) and although each example has obviously been taken from a particular discipline they are chosen because all should make reasonable sense to the average reader.

- *Manageable:* the brief for written work varies. Some pieces would be too short to be useful here, others too long to accommodate, however useful they might be, so those selected and reproduced are in the mid range, typically about 2,000 words.

Having read through this section we hope you will be encouraged to seek out more, either from fellow students or others, and to get into the habit of comparing what you do on your own topic with other work. The overall idea is to identify and avoid weaknesses and build in and on those elements that make work stand out and do the job to prompt good marks.

We are grateful to the people who allowed us to discuss their work and reproduce it here; they are mentioned specifically later in this chapter.

An example of guidelines

The educational establishment that students were attending was not a major factor in selecting these examples, except for the first one. This essay was written for an Open University (OU) course. Some may feel that is not typical so let us explain why it is included. First, it should be said at once that the standards here, of teaching, students and results is high, but it is another characteristic of the OU that makes it appropriate in this list – it is in the name. Although students do have some interactive sessions, it is in the nature of an open course that matters, including essay setting and writing, are conducted at a distance. In a university a lecturer must set an essay question and make sure that students understand the brief. Although there may be notes to guide people and some aspects of the brief may be written, usually there is an opportunity to tell students about it too and to answer questions.

At the OU this is not possible. Everything happens at a distance and essay setting must be made clear in writing and must have sufficient precision to act as a total brief. The guidelines therefore are clear and comprehensive; indeed they represent an object lesson of such guidance. So, before getting to our first example, which is from an OU student, we start by quoting some of the guidance material the OU issues. This makes a dramatically good example of what must be thought about and borne in mind prior to writing an essay and we are grateful to The Open University for permission to reproduce it here.

These guidelines are, of course, only one way of approaching this (and we are not suggesting that they take precedence over the guidance your own university provides), but all the points made here are eminently sensible and provide food for thought for any student faced with an important essay to write.

TAKE NOTE

The OU material is not here because the individual points it makes should be noted: they are sensible points but are, of course, *specific to one course offered by this institution* (so remember that your own university's version of this kind of guidance may differ). Rather it provides a clear indication of the need to always carefully follow a brief and of the kind of detail that is important if you are to deliver something that matches the brief – and which will be rated highly. It shows also how easy it can be to overlook some apparently small detail. There is a great deal of detail here; it all matters and doubtless the detail you will be faced with will be similar in nature. If attention to such detail is not in evidence then you are likely to find that this dilutes your overall standard and gets you marked down in some way.

The OU guidance

Let's go through this extract sequentially. Note that this text links to the first essay example, which is on an Art History course. Some of what follows is a verbatim quotation and some is just described (the full details being less important).

The headings that follow reflect the order of the OU instructions.

Marking criteria used on the course

This lists seven grades in the way they mark from what is called Pass 1 (A): 85–100 per cent, to Bad fail: 0–14 per cent. The way three grades are described is shown here: you can usefully have this much detail in mind before you put pen to paper as it were on an assignment of yours (another example of this categorization was given in Chapter 1).

MARKING CRITERIA USED ON THE COURSE

It is difficult to break down precisely the basis of the allocation of marks to an assignment. Each assignment is unique in the combination of qualities, strengths and weaknesses it demonstrates. Nevertheless, you might find the table of marketing criteria given below (Table 6.1) a useful guide to the general characteristics you should seek to develop in your own assignments.

TABLE 6.1

University scale score	Performance standard	General criteria applied
85–100	Pass 1 (A)	Special signs of excellence, e.g. unusual clarity, originality or coherence of argument; excellent understanding and application of course material; a deft and thoughtful use of evidence; lucid expression of ideas.
70–84	Pass 2 (B)	Approaching but not quite achieving the standards required of Pass 1. A Pass 2 answer will typically demonstrate a richer and more developed argument or analysis than Pass 3, with a clearly stated, coherent introduction and conclusion. An intelligent application (as well as choice) of evidence will also be characteristic. Relevant issues will have been identified and debated effectively. The greater the number of such features in the assignment, the higher the level in this gradation of marks.
30–39	Bare fail	More relevant content than a clear fail, but seriously marred by vagueness, error or a general apparent lack of understanding of the course or of the question set, perhaps exacerbated by weak expression.

Next the OU document sets out some overall guidelines, stressing that it is important to follow all the instructions and the importance of deadlines (and what to do if one proves impossible to hit for some tangible reason – no doubt the OU is as unlikely to give you extra time for a hangover as any other university). Then, after a few words about the role of assignments (what the OU refers to as TMAs – Tutor-marked assignments) in an overall course, it sets out some detailed instructions which are all very sensible and of general application.

TAKE NOTE

As we get into more detail, remember that this is what is said by one particular institution. We are not suggesting you follow this slavishly though the points are well made, rather that you take on board just how detailed such guidance is and read and follow whatever version of this you are given slavishly. It starts with an important point.

PLANNING YOUR TMAs

The following points are good practice in all TMAs which require an answer in the form of a continuous essay:

- Always begin by scrutinising the question you are asked: what jobs does it ask you to do and which issues does it raise? What are the key words you must bear in mind if you want to construct a relevant answer? One of the key causes of poor performance in essay writing is inadequate scrutiny of a question and the demands it makes.

- Tease out the meanings of any key words. Use the question's key issues, tasks and terms as a basis for defining and refining the structure of your essay. You need to organize your material in a way that makes the key issues and your approach to handling them highly prominent.

- Scan the section(s) of course material to which the TMA relates (bearing in mind any guidance notes provided with the TMA) to see which parts will be most relevant to the TMA you are tackling. The inclusion of irrelevant material/point in your assignment will undermine its quality.

- Make notes on these relevant sections of course material, and take care to consider how this material fits into the logic of your answer: for example, into the point – counterpoint – conclusion structure of a well-rounded argument.

- Organize your essay by making a plan and sorting your notes under headings. You can do this either way before you start writing or after you have prepared a first draft: choose whichever way suits your method of working.

- Review your notes and plan, and place your points in the most effective order possible, so that you construct a coherent argument or progression of ideas in your assignment.

- In general, you should open a new paragraph for each new substantial point you make. Announce that point clearly at the beginning of the paragraph, make clear its relationship to your preceding point and/or to the question in general (in order to ensure a coherent flow of argument throughout your essay) and devote the rest of the paragraph to amplifying and illustrating the point you make. Paragraphs which are too short (three lines or so) will not allow you to develop or illustrate sufficiently any points you make. Those which are too long (a page or so) are probably insufficiently focused.

- Make sure that the evidence you cite to support your points is appropriate and that you give a source for any quotation (see 'Presenting your TMAs' below). Remember that in many art history questions the most effective evidence will include detailed reference to a specific text or work of art.

- Begin your essay with an introduction which sets out briefly the way you have interpreted the task(s) set by an assignment and the way in which you intend to tackle the task. If the question asks you to take sides in an argument, you may wish to outline your own perspective – in support of a given proposition, against it or seeing points on both sides. Your method here will be determined by the way in which the question is worded. For example, in a 'To what extent do you agree with the following view ...' question, you will have to state clearly, at some point, the extent of your agreement or disagreement with a given point of view. Your introduction may be the best place to do this. You may wish to say, for example, that you entirely agree (or disagree) with the set proposition or that you agree in some cases but not in others. Alternatively, you could work cumulatively throughout your essay to an overall judgement stated clearly in your conclusion, but this overall judgement must be delivered at some point.

- Round off your essay with a conclusion in which you summarize your main points and restate (or state for the first time) your general response to the question posed.

- In art historical essays in particular, it is important to be careful about how you discuss your own emotional responses to works of art. Describe the qualities you observe in the things you look at and remember that feelings and emotions, while they may be experienced in front of works of art, are not properties which the works themselves have (i.e. paintings are things and don't have emotions). If you ascribe an emotional quality to a painting, you must say how and why you are making the ascription. The feeling you experience may be strong, but it will not tell us anything about your understanding of the work of art unless you can account for it in terms of qualities observable in the work. Video 2, Understanding Painting and Sculpture, explores this process.

If you are asked to discuss the relationship between form and meaning, it is not enough to describe formal elements without discussing the effects and ideas they generate. For example, 'the painting has a low viewpoint' is less effective than 'the painting's low viewpoint allows the viewer to see a greater expanse of sky and emphasizes the cloud formations and the effects of light on them, which in this case are mellow. This evokes ideas of natural harmony.' By 'meaning' we mean the ideas, feelings and associations evoked by a work of art. But these aspects must be linked tightly, in any pictorial analysis, with the specific formal aspects which generate them. What we're looking for is a close link between cause (formal aspect or feature of a work of art) and effect (meanings generated).

If you have not recently completed any essays, you may find the following a useful additional source of advice on planning essays and on study skills in general: E. Chambers and A. Northedge, *The Arts Good Study Guide*, The Open University, 1997. It is not required reading on this course, but should be easily available from bookshops. Alternatively, *Writing at University: A Guide for Students* by Phyllis Creme and Mary R. Lea, Open University Press, 1997, is a useful practical guide to the complete process of writing.

It should be clear that these points are relevant, helpful and that, topic apart, the points made are very much of general relevance for many students doing different courses. Many points made in this example are commented on in various ways in different places in the text.

In the next section the OU focuses on the presentation of work.

PRESENTING YOUR TMAs

Your TMAs should be legible. It will be difficult for a tutor to judge the force of your points or the effectiveness of your writing if he or she cannot read your writing. It will also be essential in the examination that your writing is legible. If you have a special difficulty with your handwriting which cannot be overcome by extra attention to its neatness, please contact your Regional Office to ask about the different forms of support which may be available to you in presenting both your TMAs and your exam answers. Word-processed assignments will be welcome, but this mode of presentation will not, in itself, attract extra marks. When presenting your assignment please bear in mind the following points:

(a) Word length
A word length is indicated for each assignment. It is important to work within the limit given (i) in order to ensure that you and your fellow students are working within fair and equal constraints and (ii) in order to acquire the skill in concise expression which will be essential in the exam. While tutors may show some slight leniency over observations of the word limits set for early assignments, penalties in the form of deducted marks may be applied to essays which show a significant disregard for the limits set in later assignments. It is therefore a good idea to establish as early as possible the habit of estimating how many words of your own writing typically fit on to a page. As a general rule, if your answer is severely over length you will need to edit for relevance

or reduce the detail or range of evidence and/or background description you have provided. If your answer is severely under length you may not have understood the full implications of the question and should check its wording. It is, however, possible for a shorter essay of appropriate quality to score a high grade. Please note that the word length includes quotations and references, but not your bibliography (see p. 9).

(b) Size of paper

Please use A4 paper wherever possible, as this will be compatible with the Open University stationery supplied to students and tutors.

(c) Margins

Please leave a wide margin (approximately 4 cm) in which your tutor can write comments on the script of your assignment. Some tutors prefer their students to write on alternate lines or just on one side of the paper rather than leave a wide margin. This is the kind of advice you should receive from your tutor in his or her introductory letter.

(d) Numbering pages

Please number the pages of your assignment for ease of reference for both you and your tutor.

(e) Information on each page

Make sure your name and personal identifier are shown at the top of each page of your assignment.

(f) Writing out the question

The TMA question should always be written out in full at the head of your assignments. There is no need, however, to reproduce passages of text or guidance notes supplied with TMAs.

(g) How to set out illustrations

If you wish to include photocopied or printed illustrations of visual images to which your assignment refers, please add these as an appendix. Number them clearly and add captions. Make sure there are clear references to any illustrations in the body of your essay.

(h) Underlining conventions

If you are submitting a handwritten assignment, underlining should be used as a substitute for the italics which would be used in printed text, i.e. to indicate the title of a book or painting or to emphasize a particular word.

(i) Quotations, references and bibliography

Lengthy quotations (which will be calculated as part of your total word length) should be avoided if possible. There will be times, however, when a verbatim quotation of a few words or sentences will complete or illustrate nicely a point you are making. If your quotation is very short, you might incorporate it into one of your own sentences, thus:

> The evidence does seem to support Crow's view that Watteau's art conveys an '... ambiguity of costume and status' (Crow, Painters and Public Life, p. 55).

Here, the ellipsis (represented by three dots) indicates the parts of the quoted sentence you are omitting in order to make the quotation fit grammatically, and in a way that makes sense, with your own sentence. Longer quotations should be introduced by a colon, as follows:

> The status of photography in the Victorian age influenced the public reaction to images of the nude:
>
> 'From its inception photography was discussed as a process that encompassed both technical and artistic concerns. Contemporary definitions of photography as 'truth' contradicted the concept of the nude as art. The female nude was hailed as an object of aesthetic delectations when it came to painting or sculpture, but not so with photography – a medium considered incapable of transcending of its subject.'
>
> (Smith, 'The Victorian Nude', p. 55)

What is shown here is followed by a paragraph about how, precisely, to set out references so that it is clear where material or ideas quoted in an essay originate (this was covered in Chapter 5). Every student should carefully follow the particular guidelines that they are given or they are likely to lose marks.

The briefing ends with a paragraph headed simply 'Plagiarism'. This starts: 'Every word of your essays, apart from quotations, must be your own.' Confirmation, if such were necessary, that this is something taken very seriously by every academic establishment. We have commented, firmly, on this on page 11. Let's now examine an essay written with these guidelines in mind.

Examples

Example 1

This was written by someone studying for a degree in Art History at the OU. It is about 1,700 words in length and, like the other examples here, is reproduced verbatim.

> Nicolas Poussin's *Eliezer and Rebecca*, and Claude Lorrain's *Landscape with Aeneas at Delos*. a) How do the form and content of each work contribute to its overall meaning. b) Provide some reasons why these works have acquired canonical status in western art.
>
> a) On one level, the subject of Poussin's painting reflects its biblical title. On the other, some elements of its construction might suggest it as an allegory for the Annunciation. It is also a demonstration by the artist of his classical learning and intellectual aspiration to history painting.

The most striking aspect of the picture is the arrangement of 14 brightly lit, highly coloured and delineated figures across the central part of the canvas. Like a frieze on a temple entablature, it has a kind narrative sequence and the most important characters are emphasized by having more space around them. Poussin wants to focus our attention on Eliezer and Rebecca. They are placed nearly central and close to the picture plane so that the viewer feels he is a close witness to the action. The horizontal shape of the picture, to accommodate all the figures, is given some vertical symmetry by the right pillar and the distant building rear left that also serve to frame and emphasize the main figures.

A diagonal on the right foreground from the feet of the last figure on the right passing Rebecca's toes intersects at the front of the picture with another diagonal from the feet of the two brightly lit women on the left. The effect is a foreshortening to recess the figures at the edges and to push Eliezer and Rebecca forwards. The effect of the brightly coloured clothes make the whole figure group stick out against the darker background.

The limit of the rear of the foreground plane is marked by the well delineated and subtly lighted jar on the head of women centre left set against the hazier building behind. A similar effect is performed by the pillar on the right. The background is not relevant to the story detail, buts its depiction in a grand Italiante manor and the omission of Eliezer's camels might suggest an altogether more high-minded vision by Poussin than the Genesis story.

All the women are portrayed as idealized beauties. Their style of dress, hair, and enigmatic facial features are copies from classic statuary. The hand-on-hip pose of the woman third right, and Rebecca's foot, are nearly identical to those of the *Cesi Juno* in Rome. Poussin uses subtle tones of light and shade to model the folds of the material and the anatomy beneath. We see this also on Eliezer's tunic to suggest its movement, echoing that of his left foot. Eliezer is not static but clearly approaching Rebecca.

The poses of the figures are significant. Rebecca stands out from the rather louche attitude of those on the right and the bustle and chat of those on the left. She is the most delicately drawn, the most poised, the most elegant and with embroidery on her dress; these mark her out as the 'chosen one'. The colouring also gives the same message by the strong contrast of her cool blue dress to the warm oranges and the reds to her left and right. The scene is brightly lit from the upper left. The positions of the pink and yellow women on the left and the bright illumination on their shoulders form a strong diagonal as if they are pulling the light towards the central figures. Eliezer's back is the light and his positioned to throw a shadow across Rebecca – the only strong shadow in the painting, perhaps an allegory for the presence of God. To reinforce this, Poussin has obscured the features of Eliezer's face (by convention the face of god is unknown and never shown). Finally, the interaction of the advancing Eliezer and the slightly defensive pose of Rebecca is mirrored by the words of the annunciation story '... she was troubled at his saying and cast in her mind what manner of salutation this should be.' (1).

Like Poussin, Claude has used an ancient text – Virgil's *Aeneid*, but the emphasis of the picture is less upon the characters than on the landscape. Rather than pulling things forward, the composition is designed to push our eye away from the front plane and into the landscape. The scale of the main figures near the columns indicates the viewpoint is distant and high up, giving a panoramic view. The heads of the two figures on the parapet upper right (who are drawing attention to the bas relief and the metopes) are the same size as the main group, indicating our eye level is midway between them and the main group. In the lower half of the picture the base of the trees is the focal point: a diagonal from the strong line of the bridge on the left, and another from the right connecting the hand of the soldier beneath the portico and the outstretched arm of Anius, intersect there. Further back, the line of the distant port buildings on the left, and the line of the shore opposite connect to a vanishing point in the far distance behind the trees. Finally, the line of the cornice upper right extends our eye out into the distant pale sky.

There is about the picture an atmospheric sense of tranquillity and peace. The poses of the figures betray no sense of urgency; nor can we interpret their facial expressions, they suggest instead a sense of quietly civilized behaviour on a warm and peaceful afternoon. Goats graze drowsily in the middle distance while their keeper rests beneath the trees. Our eye wants to amble around the picture as if Claude invites us to stroll through his landscape like the woman with her child and dog on the bridge crossing a gently flowing stream. What Claude seems to want us to appreciate is the feeling of timeless harmony between man, nature and the geometry of classical architecture – an arcadian landscape.

The effect of the muted colours is very significant to the sense of calm. The pale greys, greens, blues and sand colours help the landscape recede away. There are no loud primary colours to disturb the eye or the senses. The only red is on the Aeneas's tunic, possibly to identify him, but even this is very pale and only catches the eye in passing, as do the blues on the other figures. The light is from the middle left, but not so brilliant as to cast deep shadows or cause any glitter or dazzle. While the architecture on the left front, the foreground stonework and the figures shows careful linear brushwork, the landscape, sea, sky and distant buildings are more painterly and less defined giving the effect of a warm haze. It has a textural feel more akin to the atmosphere of a watercolour painting.

(b) Those behind the foundation of the Academie royale Paris in 1648, notably Charles Le Brun, sought to elevate painting and sculpture from the craft roots of the Maitrise guild to that of a an intellectual and liberal art to rank alongside ancient epic poetry. This elevation led to the promotion of a hierarchy of genres at the head of which was history painting.

Writing in 1669, Andre Felibien, a consultant to the Academie and therefore influential in furthering its ambitions for high art, suggested the artist could show '... the force, nobility and greatness of his art' through the depiction of the human figure ('Gods most perfect work on earth') in 'legendary tales and allegorical compositions' (2). This included biblical subjects. He saw such art as a teaching tool – 'we must... educate pupils accordingly' (2) – which could help institutionalize and perpetuate such values. Underlying these values was the cultural reverence for the art, architecture and literature of the ancient Greeks and Romans. This was the classical tradition stretching back through the Renaissance and with roots from Plato in 400 BC. Classical statuary was held to represent the very zenith of form and beauty in nature and was, consequently, the very best model for artists to study. The history painter, therefore, was not merely a technician but a master of grand intellectual design and concept.

The role of the Academie must also be seen within the context of the cultural, political and economic situation of the mid 17th century. The patrons of art where largely those with wealth, learning and power – the king, his court and the Roman Catholic church. Poussin counted amongst his patrons both Louis XIV and Cardinal Rospigliosi. France at that time was becoming a significant military and political force and in this climate high art was symbolic of civilization, power and glory, not only to the state and its aspirations, but also to those associated with it. Through its emphasis on history painting the Acadamie was an intellectual elite in tune with the system upon whose patronage it relied.

In the context of the aspirations of the Academie in 1648 we can see how and why a history painting like *Eliezer and Rebecca* quickly acquired canonical status. Poussin's position was reinforced by 17th century theorists such as Bellori and Felibien.

The position of Claude's picture in 1672 appears different. In spite of its classical references it is, in essence, merely a landscape, next to bottom in the hierarchy of genres of the time. However, canons and hierarchies are always subject to debate, evolution and change due to shifting political and social ideas. Eventually each genre contained its own canon and the old hierarchy withered. A good example of this is the popularity 100 years later of Chardin's genre and still life work. The portability of smaller work (and Claude's painting is relatively small) became attractive to private collectors who replaced state and church patronage. By the start of the 19th century, Claude's work was clearly canonical and much revered by J.M.W. Turner.

Notes and sources

1   Gospel of St Luke. Chap. 1 vv 29
2   Andre Felibien, from the preface to *Conference de L'Academie Royale de Peinture et de Sculpture*, as printed in *Art and its Histories*, ed. Steve Edwards pp. 34–36

Bibliography

1   OU Book 1. *Academies, Museums and Canons of Art*. pp. 1–187
2   OU *Study Handbook* 1
3   Video 1 and 2
4   TV1 and audio 1 – part 1 and 2.

You will note that the bibliography listed above refers mainly to specific OU material. However, it is reproduced here as an integral part of the essay.

Marking

This received 83 per cent and was described as being based on sound analysis and making detailed and relevant points. The student was verbally advised that the quality of writing was good, the sequence and structure worked well and the essay accurately addressed the question. Other comments on what was the first essay by the student at the start of his course related to specific details of the two paintings discussed and to points that could have been added or expanded (the details do not matter here).

The correct emphasis perhaps comes over time and from the way earlier work is commented on, indeed a learning process in this respect seems to have been in evidence here as the next essay by this student received a higher mark (85 per cent)!

Even someone unfamiliar with the topic can appreciate that this represents a job well done; looking back to the essay-writing checklist may also be useful in helping link this and other examples to your own tasks.

Example 2

Our second example features an essay from a student studying a degree in Management at Anglia Ruskin University. This is a little longer than the first (c. 3,000 words) and again the topic should make sufficient sense despite being read out of context. This time the tutor's comments are reproduced verbatim.

INTEGRATED HUMAN RESOURCE MANAGEMENT
  Module Code: BD415007S
A Critical Evaluation of the HR Function, What it Really Contributes, its Strengths and Where it Needs to Develop
Path: MA Human Resource Management
SID: 0924656/1

Tutor: Jonathan Smith

January 2011

TABLE OF CONTENTS

Critically Evaluate the HR Function. What Does it Really Contribute, What Are its Strengths and Where Does it Need to Develop?

1 Introduction

The cliché 'people are our greatest assets' and the fact that employees are the critical element in a firm's success have become common wisdom (Hall, 2005). There is a broad agreement among scholars and practitioners alike that maximizing the potentials of human resources is central to organizational effectiveness and performance in the 21st Century global market place of intense competition. Indeed, the management of human capital in organizations has become a central factor in maintaining and improving organizational performance (Lambooij et al 2006: 1).

Given the above, there is therefore, the critical need to maximally harness the potentials of employees through effective HR interventions by appropriately aligning the overall business strategy with the HR strategy for maximum productivity. As Delaney and Huselid (1996) rightly note, the way in which an organization manages people can influence its performance.

However, the relationship between effective Human Resource Management (HRM) function and organizational performance has remained a vexed issue among scholars, managers and even among HR practitioners. While some commentators (e.g. Delaney & Huselid, 1996; Abella, 2004) argue that effective HR practices remain the kernel for achieving competitive advantage, others (e.g. Guest, 1997, 1998) are sceptical of this claim and question the basis of linking HR practices to organizational performance. An assessment of recent literature on the subject matter indicates that the controversy still rages.

It is against this backdrop and in recognition of the costs (both implicit and direct) associated with the HR function, that this paper critically evaluates the HR function, with a view of highlighting its contributions to organizational effectives and performance. It argues that there are empirical evidences (e.g. Hyde et al, 2006; Katou & Budhwar, 2010; Hertog et al, 2010; etc) to suggest that there are clear linkages between effective HR function and organizational effectiveness and improved performance, but the greatest challenge remains how to quantify these contributions. The paper also notes that a lot can still be done to maximize these linkages and contributions; and while not pretending to have any 'best practice' paradigm, it concludes that for this to happen (i.e. maximizing HR's contributions), HR must critically re-examine its functions and position itself to play a more strategic role in strengthening organizational capabilities and competencies and be proactive in its approach (Abella, 2004).

2 The HR function: a critical assessment

There is no consensus among scholars and practitioners alike on what precisely constitutes the HR function, neither are there any univocal definitions. However, there is a general agreement that it is a critical business function. At its most basic level, the HR function comprises all the roles and activities performed by HR in organizations towards achieving organizational strategic objectives. Building organizational capability is HR's heartland (Holbeche, 2009).

A critical assessment of the HR function, clearly indicates that it has evolved continuously over the years. Traditionally, it was largely administrative in nature, comprising what is now seen as transactional aspects of HR, such as recruitment and selection, induction of new staffs and maintaining of staff records (Markington & Wilkinson, 2008). Foot and Hook (2002: 3) identified these transactional HR function as follows:

Recruitment and selection: concerned with the

Training and development

Human resource planning

Provision of contracts

Provision of fair treatment

Provision of equal opportunities

Assessing performance of employees

Employee counselling

Employee welfare

Payment and reward of employees

Health and safety

Discipline and dealing with grievances

Dismissal and Redundancy.

However, the increasing global nature of competition requires that firms maximally utilize all their available resources (finance, marketing, HR etc) as a means of achieving a competitive advantage (Wright et al, 1998). Subsequently, there was great emphasis on the alignment of all functional activities of the firm, including HR toward achievement of strategic objectives. The HR function was therefore, expected to support the organization in achieving high performance people management and managing the changes required to improve efficiency, even as many advocated a more strategic role for the function (Wright et al, 1998; Abella, 2004).

In the same vein, changes in the nature of managerial work over the years, coupled with new models of organizational flexibility, technological developments and the changing world of work, means that the contemporary HR function is remarkably different from what it was two or three decades ago. As Caldwell (2003: 984) rightly argues, 'the emergence of HRM as a panacea for integrating business strategy and people management has exposed personnel practitioners to a new set of role demands, professional challenges and management expectations; even as there have become greater involvement of line managers. The CIPD (2006: 6) aptly sums the situation thus:

The HR function has changed substantially from our original understanding of what an HR function should look like, with increased segmentation, devolution and outsourcing of departments. The HR function is transforming its focus from the management of human resources to the development and maintenance of organizational effectiveness.

Several works have attempted to capture this new set of demands, and the changing HR function. Marchington & Wilkinson (2008: 179), for instance, summarizes the 'new' HR functions to include: administration, negotiation, legal expertise, organizational development and business partner.

Similarly, Storey (1992) has long ago identified what Caldwell (2003: 987) refers to as the fourfold typologies of HR function based on the basis of two bi-polar dimensions: *intervention* versus *non-intervention* and *strategy* versus *tactics*. These roles are: advisors, service provider, regulators and change makers. See Table 6.2.

TABLE 6.2   The Fourfold Typologies of HR function

• Service Provider: provides line managers specific HR assistance and support as required. Handmaidens.
• Regulator: formulates, promulgates and monitors the observance of HR policy and practice.
• Change makers: actively pushes forward processes of culture change and organisational transformation.

SOURCE: Caldwell (2003).

However, the Ulrich's (1998) model, perhaps, provides the most succinct systematic frameworks for capturing the contemporary HR function. Ulrich (1998) cited by Caldwell (2003, p. 986) insists that HR professionals must overcome the traditional marginality of the personnel function by embracing a new set of roles as champions of competitiveness in delivering value; and identifies the following as the 'contemporary' HR function: employee advocate, functional expert, human capital developer, strategic partner and HR leader (CIPD, 2006). See Fig 6.1.

An expansion of the responsibilities associated with the above HR roles, clearly reveal the contributions of the HR function to organizational effectiveness and performance. Using the Ulrich model as a guide, the next few paragraphs critically analyses these HR roles and its functions with the aim of highlighting and quantifying its contributions to organizational performance. It is instructive to point however, that despite its limitations, the Ulrich model has been adopted to ensure lucidity.

3 Contributions of the HR function to organizational effectiveness and performance: a critical overview

As already noted, there is a continuing debate on what the HR function really contributes to organizations. The most fundamental issue remains how to understand how HRM practices

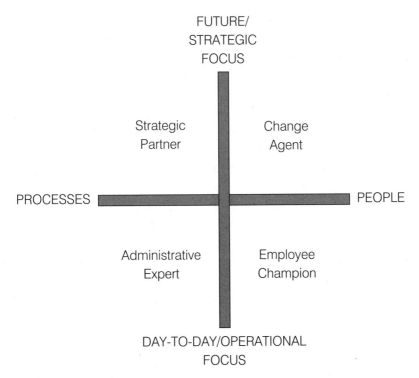

FIGURE 6.1   Ulrich's four roles of HR professionals
SOURCE: Caldwell (2003: 987)

impact on performance (Hall, 2004). Consequently, producing an unequivocal response to the question 'what does HRM really contribute to organizational performance?' has remained elusive (Guest, 1987, cited in Tyson, 1998). Indeed, many (e.g. Hall, 2005) have questioned the usefulness of HR to organizations.

The plethora of criticisms against the HR function includes what some analysts have characterized as the lack of business awareness, lack of practical relevance of most of its policies and obsession with rules (Hall, 2005; Lee, 2003). Banjoko (2007) had even characterized the function as nothing but a fad.

Similarly, the function has also been criticized for adding costs, instead of value to the organization, because it does not really prove its contributions in financial terms and returns on investment. It is this line of reasoning that led Banjoko (2007) to conclude that what organizations need are not effective HR departments, but effective line managers, arguing that delivering organizational reality and objectives is the responsibility of line managers and executives, and not HR.

However, a critical and objective assessment of the function seems to suggest otherwise and indicates that it indeed, adds value and contributes to organizational performance in no small way. In specific terms and adapting the Ulrich model as a guide, as an employee advocate, the HR function maximizes employee commitment and contribution (Caldwell, 2003). It does this by acting as a voice for employees both in representing their concerns to senior managers, empathizing with them, and in working to improve their contributions, commitment and engagement (Marchington & Wilkinson, 2008: 187). As a result, employees are highly motivated and committed to organizational objectives, which in turn translate to low staff turnover, efficient work force and increased productivity. Tsui et al (1997) corroborate this view, when they argue that an employer that takes care of its employee is most likely to get the best out of them. Relying on the Mutual-investment model, they affirm that when employer looks after her employees, her employees will look after her. When an employer signals that she takes care of the well-being of her employees, employees will react with more good will, commitment and willingness to corporate (Lamboij et al, 2006).

In a similar vein, as a functional expert, HR constantly improves organizational efficiency by re-engineering the HR function and other work processes (Caldwell, 2003: 987). As Marchington and Wilkinson (2008: 187) have noted, 'HR is a profession that possess a body of knowledge about the management and development of people which can assist both them and the organization to make effective decisions'. This is especially true in today's global economy where all that matters is 'knowledge'. In this capacity, the HR function contributes to 'foundational' practises such as recruitment and selection, promotions and rewards/remuneration, as well as to other areas of business operations such as work process design, organizational structures, internal communication, salary administration, employee records, redundancies and so on (Marchington & Wilkinson, 2008). Undoubtedly, without these functions, no organization will survive. Perhaps, it is the meticulous way in which HR handles these functions that some analysts have characterized as obsession with rules.

Further, the HR function also contributes in delivering organizational transformation and culture change (Caldwell, 2003). As a human capital developer and 'change agents', the function fulfils this responsibility by actively building and maintaining a corporate culture that embraces people development (Abella, 2004: 39). In line with the concept of Human Capital Theory (Becker, 1964) and the Resource Based View of organizations (Barney & Wright, 1998), an organization that constantly updates the skills, knowledge and competencies of its workforce (the learning organization) through an effective HR driven learning and development strategy, will definitely have a sustainable advantage over its competitors. Devanna (1984) supports this argument, when he affirms that HRM and highly skilled employees are now often seen as major factors differencing between successful and unsuccessful organization, more important than technology or finance in achieving a competitive advantage.

What is more, the HR function equally contributes to the formulation and effective implementation of business strategies. As 'strategic/business partners', it has shown itself capable of playing a critically central role in the successful formulation and execution of business strategies and in meeting customers' needs (Caldwell, 2003). As Marchington and Wilkinson (2008: 188) rightly noted, by being actively involved in crafting strategies that help to align customer needs and organizational approaches; and 'leading on how to raise the standards of strategic thinking for the management team, the HR function plays a significant part in creating the *systems* and *processes* that help deliver organizational success'.

From the forgoing analyses, it is evident that the contributions of the HR function to organizational performance are wide-ranging and indeed, critical. This is most evident in its capacity to:

- Motivate and engage employees for maximum commitment and productivity.
- Recruit and develop highly skilled and competent workforce to deliver business objectives.
- Deliver appropriate reward strategies to match employee contributions and enhance performance.
- Engage in functional and technical roles such as redundancy handling and grievance/ disciplinary procedures with subsequent cost savings for organizations.
- Partner with senior managers to formulate and implement appropriate strategies to achieve business objectives.

The forgoing are all characteristics of the high commitment HR approach. Therefore, it is plausible to argue that organizational performance is centrally hinged on the effectiveness of the HR function, particularly the high commitment model. Corroborating this assertion, Devana (1984: 41) argues that:

Performance is a function of all the HR components: selecting people who are the best able to perform the jobs defined by the structure; appraising their performance to facilitate the equitable distribution of rewards; motivating employees by linking reward to high level of performance; and developing employees to enhance their current performance at work as well as to prepare them to perform in positions they may hold in the future.

Fig 6.2 gives a simple graphic representation of the HR-performance link.

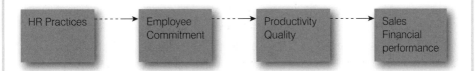

FIGURE 6.2   The HR-performance link
Adapted from Guest (2007)

Yet, it must be admitted that line managers are indeed, very critical to organizational performance. Delivering the reality should therefore, be a shared task between HR and line managers and executives. As Holbeche (2009) rightly pointed out:

It is line managers who are key communication gateways, whose priorities influence how people spend their time, whose management styles have a direct bearing on the climate for performance. It is managers, executives and leaders at all levels who model values, provide clarity of direction, create employee engagement and change-ability.

4 Conclusion

It is evident from the foregoing analysis, that the HR function is very crucial to organizational survival and gaining of competitive advantage. Although with several daunting challenges, especially its inability to quantify its contributions in monetary terms and ROI, the function remains central in maintaining the psychological contract and affects the knowledge, skills, abilities, attitudes and behaviours of employees; even as it continuously contributes to effective strategy formulation and implementation, and therefore, ultimately affects organizational performance (Lamboij, 2006).

It must be acknowledged however, that despite these sterling contributions, the HR function still needs to improve in certain areas, so as to position itself to make more well-informed strategic contributions to organizational success in line with changing demands and exigencies of the business environment. As more and more is expected of employees, the HR function must be more than an administrative arm of an organization and be increasingly involved in facilitating growth, productivity and profitability (Abella, 2006: 37).

5 Recommendations and implications for HR

Given the above, the HR function, must therefore, become more strategic and proactive in its approach and tailor its contributions to support the realization of the strategic business objectives. One major way of achieving this, is through the Strategic Business Partner approach and effective workforce planning (CIPD, 2009). As noted earlier, one of the greatest criticism always levelled against the HR function, is that of lack of alignment and proper integration with the overall business strategy. While this argument is not totally valid or totally false, there is nonetheless, the need to properly align HRM with organisational strategy (*strategic fit/vertical integration*), and the alignment of various HR functions such as career opportunities, training, appraisal and so on, with the organization (*internal fit/horizontal integration*) (Baron & Kreps, 1999).

Similarly, apart from striving to achieve strategic and internal fit, and supporting the organization in achieving high performance people management, as well as managing the changes required to improve organizational efficiency, the HR function needs to review its own performance to ensure that it is efficient and effective (EO, 2007). This kind of re-assessment is crucial if the HR function is to continue delivering quality service, attain a return on investment (ROI) and further prove its contributions (Abella, 2004). As *The Employers' Organisation* (2007: 1) has noted, a review of the effectiveness of the function will look at whether:

- The function's service plan (i.e. HR strategy) reflects organizational need and appropriate strategy for the deployment, management and development of the workforce is in place. Simply put, do we have the appropriate HR strategy?

- There is appropriate HR leadership so that people issues are considered at the outset of any organizational change.

- The current HR function organizational structure and the HR job roles reflect and meet service needs.

- The processes and systems used ensure that administrative and reporting tasks are delivered in a timely and efficient manner.

- There is an effective interface between the HR function and managers, employees. Trade unions and potential employees and all parties are clear about their roles and responsibilities in relation to the service provided.

- HR staff have the relevant competencies and capabilities to deliver what is required.

- Performance is appropriately managed and service delivery changes are made in a timely manner; even as there should be a clear strategy for evaluating the above.

This review should be systematic and evaluative, and can be done independently by the HR function or in a wider organizational context by critically auditing the current system and job roles, benchmarking against other HR functions and consultations with key stakeholders, including line managers, employees, trade unions and HR staff (EO, 2007: 1).

In addition, there is also the need to properly address certain strategic HR issues such as: the responsibility of the HR function, responsibility of line managers with regards to HR issues and technological requirements to support the growing responsibilities of the HR function in a rapidly changing world (CIPD, 2007; Abella, 2004). As Abella (2004: 38) succinctly puts it:

> In order for the HR function to move from the backroom to the boardroom, HR issues must be addressed, and the role of line managers must evolve into that which accommodates an increasing involvement in developing solutions to address the concerns of their people.

Undoubtedly, the foregoing will re-engineer the HR function and make it a more strategic contributor, greatly improve services, lead to increased business focus and profoundly reduce costs (CIP, 2007).

Given the attendant benefits of the strategic business partner approach, it is plausible to argue that maximizing the strategic contributions of the HR function and the need to become strategic business partners should be a primary pursuit of HR practitioners. While this is desirable, the recognition that less strategic and administrative functions of HR are nonetheless critical for organizational success, means that emphasize should also be on how to improve the efficacy and utility of these non-strategic and 'traditional' functions as well. The challenge therefore, is how to strike a balance between developing an effective HR strategy and policies; and contributing to business strategy on one hand, and providing support to line managers and HR administrators on the other. The implication therefore, is for the HR function to be both *transactional* and *transformational* (CIPD, 2007; Abella, 2004).

References

Abella, V. O., 2004. The HR function of the future. *The SGV Review*. (March), pp. 36–41

Banjoko, S. A., 2007. *Human resource management: an expository approach.* Ibadan: Oluseyi Press

Barney, J., 1991. Firm resources and sustained competitive advantage. *Journal of Management,* 17(1), pp. 99–120

Becker, B., & Gerhart, B., 1996. The impact of human resource management on organisational performance: progress and prospects. *The Academy of Management Journal,* 39(4) August. pp. 779–801 (Online). Available at: http://links.jstor.org/sici?sici=001-4273%28199608 [Accessed 13 November 2010]

Becker, G. S., 1964. *Human Capital: A theoretical and empirical analysis, with special reference to education.* Chicago, University of Chicago Press

Caldwell, R., 2003. The changing roles of personnel mangers: old ambiguities, new uncertainties. *Journal of Management Studies,* 40(4) (June), pp. 983–1011

Cooke, F. L., 2000. Human resource strategy to improve organisational performance: a route for British firms? ESRC future of work programme, Working Paper 9 (October)

Delaney, J. T. & Huselid, M. A., 1996. The impact of human resource management practices on perceptions of organisational performance. *Academy of Management Journal,* 39(4), pp. 949–68

Employer's Organisation (EO)., 2007. The people implication of the efficiency agenda: the HR function and efficiency. (Advice Booklet)

Foot, M., & Hook, C., 2002. *Introducing human resource management.* Harlow, Essex: Pearson Education

Guest, D., 1997. Human resource management and performance: a review and research agenda. *The International Journal of Human Resource Management,* 8(3), pp. 263–76

Guest, D., 1998. Beyond HRM: commitment and the contract culture, in M. Marchington & P. Sparrow (eds.) *Human resource management: the new agenda,* London: Financial Times, Pitman

Hall, L., 2005. HRM practices and employee and organisational performance: a critique of the research and Guest's model. Research working paper

Hertog, F. D., Iterson, A. V., Christain, M., 2010. Does HRM really matter in bringing about strategic change? Comparative action research in ten European steel firms. *European Management Journal,* 28(1) (Feb.), pp. 14–24

Holbeche, L., 2009. Building high performance – the key role for HR. *Impact,* 20

Huselid, M. A., Jackson, S. E., & Schuler, R. S., 1997. Technical and strategic human resource management effectiveness of firm performance. *Academy of Management Journal,* 40(1) (February), pp. 171–88. (Online). Available at: http://www.jstor.org/stable/257025 [Accessed 13 November 2010]

Hyde, P., et al. 2006. Improving health through human resource management: mapping the territory. (Research report) London: CIPD

Katou, A. A., & Pawan, S. B., 2010. Causal relationship between HRM policies and organisational performance: evidence from the Greek manufacturing sector. *European Management Journal,* 28(1) (Feb.), pp. 25–29

Lamboij, M., et al. 2006. Human resource practices and organisational performance: can the HRM-performance linkage be explained by the cooperative behaviours of employees? *The International Review of Management Studies,* 17(3), pp. 223–40. (Online). Available at: http://www.hamppverleg.de/ [Accessed 10 November 2010]

Marchington, M., & Wilkinson, A., 2008. *Human resource management at work: people management and development,* 4th ed. London: CIPD

The Chartered Institute of Personnel and Development (CIPD), 2005. HR strategy: creating the framework for people management. London: CIPD. (Online). Available at: http://www.cipd.co.uk [Accessed 10 November 2010]

The Chartered Institute of Personnel and Development (CIPD), 2007. The changing HR function: *Survey Report* (September). London: CIPD. (Online). Available at: http://www.cipd.co.uk [Accessed 10 November 2010]

Tsui, A., 1990. A multiple constituency model of organizational effectiveness: An empirical examination at the human resource subunit level. *Administrative Science Quarterly,* 35, pp. 458–83.

Tyson, S., 1998. How HR knowledge contributes to organisational performance. *Human Resource Management Journal,* 9(3), pp. 42–53

Wright, P. M., et al. 1998. Strategy, core competence, and HR involvement as determinant of HR effectiveness and defining performance. *Human Resource Management* 37(1) (Spring), pp. 17–29

The tutor's comments are presented in a neat format and reproduced in their entirety in Table 6.3.

TABLE 6.3   Integrated HRM assignment (3,000 words)

SID NO: 924656   DATE: 11/1/11

Introduction	A clear and engaging introduction to both the report and topic has been provided. – The introduction has been well written.
Critical evaluation of issues including use of the literature to support arguments	Clear evidence of extensive wider reading and good use of literature in report including some powerful quotations. – A good understanding of this literature demonstrated in a sophisticated and strategic level analysis. – Evidence of an objective and critical evaluation (e.g. page 5). – The relevance of some elements in the main body of the report could have been made a little clearer.
Conclusions and recommendations	Conclusions and recommendations are provided which are clear and flow from the main body of the report. – The recommendations are rather long for this short report and could have been made a little more succinct.
Presentation and structure of the report including written expression and referencing	Professionally produced report. – Clear structure with useful sub-headings to guide the reader. – Referenced well using the Harvard System. – Extensive range of sources used including academic journal articles. – Good use of diagrams and tables. – Report is very clear and easy to read. – A sophisticated writing style.

Tutor:

Note: There was no exact mark in this example, but it is clear that this was regarded as a good piece of work that was well presented and followed its brief. If you want to analyse it further you can refer back and look at it alongside the checklist on page 92; indeed you can do that for any of the essays where you think this would be useful.

Example 3

The following essay was written by Benjamin Coombs, a History student at the University of Kent. It scored 73 per cent. It is just over 2,000 words, plus references.

EXPLAIN THE COLLAPSE OF THE NAPOLEONIC EMPIRE IN 1814–1815

Introduction

The fall of Napoleon Bonaparte in 1814 and then again in 1815 can be attributed to a number of different but connected factors. There was the social and economic situation at home. The numerous campaigns and the on-going requirement for more and more men resulted in both political and military factors. And finally there was Napoleon himself. As with all great and renowned leaders they have their remarkable strengths but their flaws can sometimes be serious enough to eventually contribute to their downfall.

Social and Economic Factors

By the end of 1810, the Napoleonic Empire reached its territorial peak and had spread over 293,000 square miles with 44 million inhabitants. But beneath this apparent stability lay the deep roots of weakness and the early signs of a regime in trouble. Conscription and financial pressures continued to foster resentment and added to Napoleon's unpopularity. The occupation of Rome and the banishment of Pope Pius VII resulted in bitter hostility from devout Catholics throughout Europe and particularly those in France. Budget deficits and tax increases resulted in recession and the Continental Blockade was causing a shortage of raw materials which harmed industrialists and grain shortages provoked bread riots.

As a result of these problems Napoleon was losing support among the notables which were his main pillar of support up to his first abdication in 1814, although opposition to his rule at this time was silent.[i] The Spanish campaign was a massive drain on resources, the disastrous Russian campaign in 1812 and defeat at Leipzig in 1813 led to a desperate search for recruits totalling more than a million men.[ii] This lost him much loyalty and respect from the population at large. By now the nation wanted peace and displayed either apathy or passive resistance towards government attempts to mobilize for war on the home front. Taxes remained unpaid, requisition orders were ignored and new conscripts were slow to come forward. The civilian population were intimidated and dispirited with most offering no resistance to the advancing allied troops through their land. The only exception to this was when they were confronted with the marauding activities of the Cossacks and Prussians then the peasants begin to retaliate. As the Allied armies were approaching Paris itself Napoleon's Marshals refuse to serve him anymore and he abdicated.[iii]

Political Factors

There were irreconcilable differences between Napoleon and the other European rulers. On the one hand, Napoleon genuinely desired for acceptance and not just for his military prowess. His marriage to the daughter of the Austrian Emperor in 1809 demonstrated an attempt to be accepted by European royalty. On the other hand he was not prepared to grant a partnership. His attitude towards diplomatic relations was to use further force to overcome any resistance to his treaties.

The invasion if Russia in 1812 was largely attributed to Napoleon's desire to force Alexander I back into supporting the Continental Blockade against Britain as agreed in the Treaty of Tilsit. He failed to grasp the idea that for conquest to be effective and more importantly long lasting there must be reconciliation. For an ongoing relationship to prosper, both conqueror and conquered needed to extract concessions from each other. As a result, Napoleon's conquests only created resentment and incentive for revolt when the opportunity presented itself. This was demonstrated when the Allies put aside their collective differences to join forces to overthrow Napoleon after his retreat from Russia. As an example, Austria had to be subdued five times the last three of which were as a result of unacceptable treaties.[iv] What becomes apparent is that his fall was arguably more political than military. Napoleon's sheer reluctance to accept any peace terms in the hope of military victory sometime later finally forced those closest to him to rise up against him.[v]

Following Napoleon's return to France in 1815 his political beliefs appeared to have dramatically changed. The immediate return to his previous autocratic rule was clearly out of the question. Before he even reached Paris he signalled his desire to govern France constitutionally in accordance with the interests and will of the nation. Napoleon was therefore torn between either the Jacobin and revolutionary tendencies of 1793 or compromise with the liberals by bettering the program put forward by Louis XVIII's charter on liberties.

He decided on the latter but this was still unsatisfactory as it alienated the so called 'patriots' by leaning towards aristocracy and annoyed the liberal 'notables' by restoring manhood suffrage. The French people had acknowledged the return of the Bourbons without much enthusiasm but accepted the change as it ended the war. Napoleon's return would only be tolerated for as long as he kept away from basic Revolutionary ideals regarding land and property. He therefore adopted the program similar to that introduced by Louis XVIII before his flight to Belgium. This would consist of a constitutional monarchy based on a complete freedom of expression and a two chamber parliament with an elected lower chamber and hereditary peerage. A long time liberal opponent to Napoleon, Benjamin Constant was asked to draw up the *Acte Additionel*. Constant seemed convinced that Napoleon was sincere about giving the people liberty, free elections, ministerial freedom of action, free discussion and a free press. It has been suggested that Napoleon was caught in an impossible position between his own nature and habits and that demanded by the situation. He was effectively no longer his previous self. Others were more sceptical and believed that he returned as much the despot as before he left and that his lust for conquest was as strong as ever. The *Acte* was not a new constitution but as its name implies it was just an addition to the existing one. What seems evident was that the *Acte* was merely a stalling tactic to satisfy public opinion following his return and to secure the support of the liberals without whom he would not have been able to unite the country against the coming Allied attack. It was extremely likely that Napoleon would return France to a dictatorship once the time was right.[vi]

Military Factors

Following the battles up 1807 Napoleon had been able to defeat his enemies on the ground, whether they were Austrians, Prussians or Russians. The cost of these victories was the loss of many experienced and disciplined troops. When the new recruits went into battle they were by comparison largely untrained and sometimes unreliable. Napoleon's army was becoming increasingly more cosmopolitan with the introduction of foreign troops in large numbers filling the ranks. As a result of these changes, his army no longer had the right level of discipline to sustain attacks that had been so successfully carried out previously. He therefore had to adapt his tactics to rely more on artillery attacks with larger columns of men being crudely thrown at the enemy line with less regard for casualty rates as before. All these factors led to an increasing need for more troops and a greater drain on France's male population. As his armies became larger, his overall grip on its operations began to lessen and effective control was more difficult to achieve. In Napoleon's absence from Spain for example, the local commander left in charge was unable to cope with the requirements placed upon him in running this territory. As a result, the Spanish campaign was a constant drain on Napoleon's military resources requiring more and more men. The glorious victories in early campaigns meant that commanders were less likely to think on their own feet as they automatically expected Napoleon's strategies to give them victory. Their only duty was to obey the Emperor's commands upon receiving them.[vii]

Although he had clear initial advantages over the rest of Europe, Napoleon lost the initiative as the Allies began to adjust to his strategy and battlefield tactics and capitalized on the number of blunders caused by overconfidence and arrogance. He was eventually faced with equally large armies in the field when the cream of his forces had already been depleted and war weariness was starting to take its toll at home. By 1813, the Allies had learnt how to cope with Napoleon's surprise attacks and adopted his doctrine of avoiding battle until the decisive moment presented itself with superior numbers. By 1814 only forty percent of Napoleon's forces were Frenchmen. The rest came from Italy, Germany, Poland and Spain. It was becoming disunited and less harmonized by the time his enemies were starting to mass in greater numbers.[viii]

Personal Factors

Perhaps one of Napoleon's largest character flaws was his inability to accept peace terms in favour of his belief that total victory was still achievable. In November 1813, he rejected the terms offered by the Austrian foreign minister which would have preserved his rule in France as well as Belgium, Holland, the left bank of the Rhine and much of Italy. As the Allies were approaching France, subsequent peace offerings which would have maintained France's natural boundaries and frontiers of 1792 were again rejected by Napoleon who wanted to continue the fight. Napoleon was unable to comprehend that the coalition could remain united which was demonstrated in his defeat at Leipzig in 1813.

The Austrian Chancellor, Metternich stated that 'the habit of despising the means and capabilities of his adversaries was one of the principle causes of this downfall.'[ix] By 1814 and in the face of a numerically superior united enemy for the first time, Napoleon fell victim to supreme egotism and inflexibility with an unwillingness to face facts. Before the Treaty of Tilsit, France's greatest military asset was clearly the leadership of Napoleon himself. After Tilsit, this arguably became their greatest liability. This was where he effectively lost all sense of caution believing nothing was impossible or beyond the scope of his capabilities. Napoleon could never delegate authority effectively or consider the training of a suitable successor. The relaying of the principles of his genius to his marshals was very rarely attempted thereby producing a gap between his own strategy and the actual tactics employed by his subordinates in the field.[x]

His return in 1815 was partly down to public suspicions regarding the reinstallation of a Bourbon monarchy. Upon his return it was possible that Napoleon was no longer seeking European conquest and would have not taken up arms again had it not been for the Allies reaction to his return. It is difficult to know for sure, but given his tendency to always go on the offensive as demonstrated by his attack through Belgium in June of that year, the Allies were not prepared to allow Napoleon to gain the upper hand and again threaten their territories. They therefore began mobilizing another coalition army to challenge his return. Napoleon abdicated for a second time four days after the decisive battle at Waterloo.

Conclusion

It could be argued that the only reason why Napoleon's regime collapsed in 1814 was because the Allied armies were within striking distance of Paris. Whilst this is true from the position of the Allied armies, their route would have been far more costly had the general population not let them through largely unopposed. They were fed up with the cost of war in both its financial impact upon their livelihood but also in human lives and the program of conscription to sustain ongoing conflict. Had the French people rejected the idea of Allied army occupation they could well have rallied behind Napoleon in defending the homeland. As it turned out they did not which resulted in Napoleon's Marshals and political pressure forcing an end to his Regime. Napoleon's character flaws contributed to the successive military defeats in Russia and at Leipzig together with the constant drain on resources in holding the Empire together such as in Spain and Italy. His second Regime was far different than the one he left behind in the previous year. Bearing in mind the Allied reaction to his return to power, Napoleon's days were clearly numbered. Defeat at Waterloo rather highlighted Napoleon's downfall than actually sealed it. Had Napoleon won that day the Allied armies would have been on the march again pretty soon after. It would have only been a matter of time before they removed him from power through the adoption of superior numbers and the sheer determination not to let him threaten European peace again.

Notes

[i.] A. Grab, *Napoleon and the Transformation of Europe*, pp. 197–204

[ii.] A. Brett-James, *Eyewitness Accounts of Napoleon's Defeat in Russia*, pp. 6–7 – Napoleon invaded Russia during the spring of 1812 with approximately 600,000 men. He returned in

November of that same year with no more than 25,000 men, with only about 10,000 of them being combat ready. At Leipzig the following year his army of 185,000 men faced an Allied army of 300,000. Napoleon lost 38,000 killed or wounded and a further 30,000 captured. The Spanish Campaign or the Peninsula War ran from 1808 to 1814 and cost the lives of one million people.

iii. G. Rude, *Revolutionary Europe 1783–1815*, pp. 206–20

iv. S. Lee, *Aspects of European History: 1789–1980*, pp. 26–36 & M. Fulbrook, *German History Since 1800*, p. 34

v. M. Broers, *Europe Under Napoleon 1799–1815*, pp. 234–60

vi. A. Stiles, and D. Rees, *Napoleon, France and Europe*, pp. 46–47 & Rude, op, cit., pp. 206–20

vii. Stiles & Rees, op. cit., pp. 131–35

viii. Lee, op. cit., pp. 26–36

ix. Stiles & Rees, op. cit., pp. 131–35

x. Lee, op. cit., pp. 26–36

Bibliography

Grab, A., *Napoleon and the Transformation of Europe*, (Palgrave Macmillan, 2003)

Rude, G., *Revolutionary Europe 1783–1815*, (Blackwell, 2000)

Brett-James, A., *Eyewitness Accounts of Napoleon's Defeat in Russia*, (Macmillan, 1966)

Lee, S., *Aspects of European History: 1789–1980*, (Routledge, 1988)

Stiles, A. and Rees, D., *Napoleon, France and Europe*, (Hodder & Stoughton, 2004)

Broers, M., *Europe Under Napoleon 1799–1815*, (Arnold, 1996)

Dwyer, P. (ed), *Napoleon and Europe*, (Longman, 2001)

Fulbrook, M., *German History Since 1800*, (Hodder Arnold, 1997)

Lecturer's comments (using a standard sheet split into four categories):

Content, relevance, creative engagement: An enthusiastic and interesting essay. You show a good knowledge of a variety of factors – political, military and personal. I agree about the importance of N[apoleon]'s character. I like the Metternich quotation. It is perhaps worth asking if the Napoleonic project in general was a viable one. Reference too to emerging nationalism in the empire could have been made.

Sources: V. good. Could you have made any bibliographical references?

Presentation and technical quality: ✓

General assessment: Excellent and thoughtful. Well done.

Mark: 73%

ACKNOWLEDGEMENTS

The authors would like to thank everyone who gave the permission that allowed this example section to be printed here. So thanks are due, in order of the example essays, to The Open University and Charles Proudfoot, to Anglian Ruskin University and both Dr Jonathan Smith, Senior Lecturer at the Ashcroft International Business School and his MA student Kelechi Ekuma, and to Benjamin Coombs who was at the University of Kent.

Dealing with criticism

Having considered a selection of actual essays and seen something of the kind of comments that can accompany their return to you, we review more about criticism (this was first touched on in Chapter 1) and put this in specific context. Some comments will be positive and that is rewarding, but also dictates action.

ACTION

When you receive positive comments do not just heave a sigh of relief. Note them and resolve to deploy again any approaches that are praised. This may apply to all aspects of an essay: the research that preceded it, the way the argument is presented and the quality of the writing.

Conversely, comments made about your essays may sometimes seem to focus almost exclusively on the things that are less than perfect.

TAKE NOTE

Remember that this is less a question of things that are right or wrong in a black and white sense (though sometimes this may be the case), rather a case of opinion with your lecturer's experience being considerably greater at this stage than your own. It is a natural human reaction to become defensive and 'fight back' in the face of criticism. So any conversation about an essay or resulting from comments made in writing can deteriorate into an argument and as things are banged to and fro nothing very much is achieved. Left alone, resentment can overtake a constructive approach and lead to a missed opportunity in terms of learning lessons that will help rack up the success of future essays.

Any commentary is going to spend time on difficulties – it goes with the territory so to speak – and you must be ready to deal with this. Three intentions should be uppermost in your mind in this respect, over and above a general desire to put the best complexion on everything:

1 *Achieving accuracy:* here your intention is to ensure that the right facts are considered. Before you allow yourself a response you must be clear what is being said: is a comment about content, argument or the manner in which matters are put over? It is easier to discuss specifics and questions may well be the route to identifying them. Never argue with anything but the true facts; checking what is really meant is the first step to responding to what is said in the right way.

2 *Giving an impression of objectivity:* if every criticism appears to put you into automatic defensive mode, then consideration or discussion will be unlikely to be constructive. Using an acknowledgement to position what follows is always useful. It:

   – indicates you feel there is a point to discuss (if you do not, then we are back to achieving accuracy – see above);

   – shows that you are not going to argue unconstructively;

   – makes it clear that you intend to respond in a serious and considered fashion;

   – gives you a moment to think (which may be very useful!) and sets up the subsequent discussion so that you can handle it better.

   Just a few words may be all that is necessary here. Starting with a 'yes' gives it power – 'Yes, I can see there was a problem with that' – and sounds right as you move towards learning from what is being said.

3 *Dealing with the points raised:* now the job is to deal with the matter. Mechanistically the options are few and therefore manageable. You may need to explain why a difficulty occurred, then there are two routes to handling things:

   – clarify the problem: you need to understand the nature of every comment: as was said above is it about content or your ability to explain clearly, for instance;

   – agree the difficulty: after all, there is no point in trying to argue that black is white. Most ordinary mortals have some problems somewhere with all the written work that many courses involve. If it is clear you are open to revision and change any discussion will be easier and more constructive. Resolve to let comments change your future approach: you need to make mental and actual notes of what you intend should happen next, so that constructive comments are kept in mind and act as signposts in the writing of subsequent essays.

Remember that the prime purpose of any critique is to set the scene for success in your next essay, not argue – with yourself or your tutor – about what cannot be changed. None of us can turn the clock back, but all of us can learn from experience. So the key thing to include when the discussion touches on difficulties is the lessons that have been learnt for the future.

The list of implications and actions here is considerable. Weaknesses may have crept in because of unforeseen circumstances, lack of care, a misunderstanding, an inappropriate focus or a host of other reasons; alternatively you may have made a simple slip (and only need to make a firm mental note not to let it happen again). There may be lessons to learn, but ultimately the emphasis needs to be on what happens next, and this allows a return to the most constructive elements of the critique and dialogue.

Taking practical action from criticism

It is not enough to receive the criticism from your lecturers – you need to act on it too. The same applies to things you discover for yourself. What does this mean? It means thinking about any shortcomings of your essay that have been highlighted and considering how you can improve in future. Some of the points most often raised by lecturers in feedback to students are shown in Table 6.4 overleaf.

You can also think about any lessons that you learnt during the process of writing the essay (see Table 6.5 on page 121). By explicitly reviewing how you went about it, and in particular the things that were problematic you can avoid making the same mistakes again. It is noticeable how many students repeat the same or similar mistakes in their essay writing. Part of the student learning experience is self-assessment and learning to do this effectively will not only help you improve and stand out, but will be a useful skill in the future.

TABLE 6.4   Issues raised by lecturer

Issue	Future
You failed to achieve the right balance of material.	It is all too easy to focus in on one aspect of the essay that particularly interests you, or on which there is plenty of material available in the library. However, a good and persuasive essay needs to be balanced, examining all the relevant arguments and viewpoints before coming to a conclusion.
You failed to explore the main points in sufficient detail.	More background research is required, examining a greater volume of material.
You misunderstood the question and the material in your essay is not relevant.	With care you should not make such a major mistake, but it does happen, often when students are rushing and don't have enough time to plan their essay carefully. Make sure that you understand the question before you even begin the research, let alone the writing. Clarify anything that is not clear with your lecturer at the earliest possible stage.
Your essay contains some of the right ideas, but is poorly structured so it is neither persuasive nor clear.	Your essay needs careful planning before you begin to draft it. You need to move logically from one point to the next, including evidence for all your arguments. Once it is drafted in full you need to read it and make sure it is clear and sells your interpretation. Better still, get a friend to do this for you.
Your essay includes some relevant material (and may also be well structured) but it has not answered the question, and reads like a reference book.	Remember that you need to come to some clear conclusion on the material that you research for your essay. It is not enough to just review it – your lecturers want to see how you assess and evaluate it too. Make sure that you understand the question (see above) and then plan your essay carefully so that a persuasive line of argument is built up.

ACTION

If there is one area that needs particular care it is your response to criticism. You will often know what is likely to be raised (be honest!): be ready for any such feedback and have a constructive response ready.

TABLE 6.5   Issues arising during writing

Issue	Future
You have some key material to support your own line of thinking, but you cannot use it because you don't know where it came from and have wasted a lot of time trying to track it down.	As you research your essay you will need to consult a number of different books. Make sure that you carefully record the bibliographic details of the book, *including page numbers*, so that you can easily find the material again if you need to, and can reference it clearly in your essay.
Looking at the material in the library (or writing the essay) took longer than you anticipated.	Make an earlier start on your next essay to allow sufficient time for the necessary research (or writing up).
A key book you needed was not available.	Plan further ahead. Allocate a bit of time ahead of when you plan to research and write the essay to identify what material you need and make sure that it is available, recalling items if necessary.
Halfway through your essay you realize that you are not really engaged with the topic and would prefer to write on something else.	This can happen when you are in a rush, perhaps because of pressure of deadlines, and you begin work on a topic without fully understanding the question. Make sure you at least consider all the question options before you decide which one to work on. Do not see this stage as a waste of time; getting it right at the start can save you much more time in the long run.
Halfway through your essay you become unconvinced by your own line of interpretation.	You should only begin to write your essay once you have both undertaken the necessary research and taken time to reflect on and evaluate this material. Subsequently, careful planning will make sure you know where the essay is going, and have the material you need to support your argument.

A final point here: the constructive approach commended as a response to criticism is something that can be usefully deployed in many ways, formally and informally, in everything from a one-to-one meeting with a tutor to a moment of self-reflection.

A helping hand

Before leaving this chapter there is one area to which we would like to refer back: the sense in seeking guidance along the way from your lecturer. Not asking a simple question and proceeding on a hunch or assumption can see you waste time, deliver what is judged poor work because it is based on some sort of misconception, and receive poor marks. Such questioning may only take a moment. It could be done face-to-face or by e-mail (provided your lecturer is happy to work that way). It is not suggested that every moment of the lead-up to delivering an essay is used to ask questions; if there was a need to do that it would probably worry both the lecturer and you. So choose your moment.

Many tips and pointers have been mentioned along the way and these are now summarized and extended in checklist style.

Top tips

Liaison with lecturers

Despite the fact that university is designed to prompt self-sufficiency and working independently there is no point in ploughing ahead with things in ignorance when asking would get you on the right track quickly and easily. Muddling through may not only take longer and waste time that could more usefully be applied to something else, it could also have you missing key lessons that a project is designed to give you along the way. This is true even if muddling through gets you there in the end.

The usefulness of checking with your lecturer at various stages has been pointed out in various ways earlier in the book. Here we recap and pull these thoughts together to create a comprehensive checklist of when to liaise, ask or clarify matters. It is not suggested of course that you find something to ask on all these occasions, but we say that when something needs to be asked the best general rule is to ask sooner rather than later. Lecturers will not mind you wanting to be 100 per cent clear about something (indeed it may sometimes be them that have left it less than completely clear), but they may well take a less charitable view of having to rescue you if you have made wrong assumptions and then become lost part-way into a project. So consider checking the following:

- Early on have clear in your mind how a lecturer wants things done, what standard procedures apply, for instance to timing, presentation of work and other matters that must be consistently carried out in a particular way. Also early on (and via more than one individual lecturer if necessary) make sure that you understand what resources you will be able to use: the university library and access to all those sources that are relevant for your subject, whether online or physical.

- Once projects are set, always ask if the question – what is asked and how it should be interpreted – is not clear to you. You have to have understood this accurately before you have any chance of producing appropriate and good work.

- Ask during the preparation stage if clarification or reassurance will help (especially early in your course) regarding exactly how you should proceed. This applies across a range of matters, from accessing sources of information to verifying that the sequence in which you plan to write something is sensible.

- Ask after work has been marked and comments received if they are not clear. Comments are there to help you make the next piece of written work better. If you are not clear what is meant then the comments are unlikely to be of much use in guiding you next time.

- If your results are good do not just heave a sigh of relief. Asking exactly what it is that led to a piece of work receiving high marks can also produce comments that provide useful guidance to you for the future.

There is one other situation that prompts thoughts of checking and that's examinations. When you know how you did, it would be useful to know something about why your results were as they were. By and large that's not possible, although certain kinds of mid-course exam do allow some comment. If that is the case for you, then by all means check with your lecturer.

A further thought may be useful here; see box.

TAKE NOTE

When preparing for writing examination essays make sure that you attend any revision classes or exam preparation sessions put on by your lecturers. These might include sitting past papers, advice on how to approach examinations and revision, or even timed essays.

Timed essays, which reproduce the way that an essay would have to be done in an exam, are really useful in providing practice. These classes are often not compulsory, and whilst it might seem like an extra burden when you are already busy, attending them and doing timed essay practice can make the real examinations significantly less stressful and manageable. You will be better prepared, so you should always make them a priority.

On all these occasions the answers given to your questions may be useful. Do think before you ask, however. If you emerge from every such session with both you and the lecturer clear that if you had thought for a moment you would have had the answer without asking, then your lack of thought may damage your relationship with the lecturer and also his or her opinion of you. That said, if there is a rule here it should be: if truly in doubt – ask.

READ ON ...

With these examples in mind to exemplify the many lessons covered throughout the book, we move on to a final chapter that links good essay writing and the skills that make it possible to reap the benefits it produces both immediately and in the future.

Your notes

....

....

....

....

....

....

....

....

....

....

....

....

....

....

....

....

CHAPTER 7

Looking ahead

In this chapter we look ahead at the implications of the way you handle essays. We want to show the full extent of how getting to grips with essay writing can help you. It affects not only your study and grades and ultimately the nature of the qualification you obtain, but acquiring the skill of good writing can also assist you into the future. There is a long-term opportunity here to be taken; remember that, as a popular maxim tells us, success doesn't come to you, you go to it.

The immediate benefits

Let's recap first: while noting again the contribution that careful research, analysis and preparation make, there is no doubt that being able to write well has a direct effect on your life, work and results at university. It:

● enables you to complete your work and assignments and obtain good grades;

● saves you time by enabling you to get assignments completed, and completed well, without endless uncertainty and revision;

- contributes to your being seen as having a positive profile with academic staff (and maybe others) as a serious student; this is true of everything, from putting in written work on time to the quality of work itself, and the impact of being well thought of may have wide implications;

- ultimately is a significant factor in influencing the grades you get in exams and in whatever qualification you receive as you finish your course.

As such, embracing a suitable and appropriate writing style is something well worth any effort it takes to achieve. It is important to make a good start, viewing your early efforts constructively and working to make any changes that may be necessary to achieve what you want. It may seem daunting initially, yet it is very much an area where practice makes perfect – in other words this is something that gets easier (and quicker) with practice.

Beyond that, how does this relate to the world beyond study and the world of work particularly?

TAKE NOTE

Some of what follows may seem beyond your current span of thinking. Be careful though: time goes by all too fast so what needs to be considered can change as you watch. However, if you are reading this book ahead of or early in your course, make a note to read this chapter again in the latter stages of it. We believe that doing so can be very valuable.

The wider world

Whatever you may move onto after your time at university, you are going to find that the world of work is very different from what you have been used to; if you thought the change from school to university was a shock to the system, be ready: the change to the world of work will be much greater. Not least it is competitive. Indeed this is true to such an extent that the business workplace has been described as an extension of the kindergarten sand box – but with quicksand. Other kinds of organization are not so different.

Whatever you may do, work is likely to be a major part of your life. Most people want two things from this: rewards (including financial reward) and job satisfaction. If you are going to spend a major part of your life working, then it is surely best to do something you like. Remember what the journalist Katherine Whitehorn once said: 'The best career advice to give the young is: find out what you like doing and get someone to pay you for doing it' – perhaps good advice at any age. This is important in terms of the work that you choose, or as sometimes happens, that you fall into, and also in ensuring that you maximize the job satisfaction and rewards you get from whatever you do.

We do not choose and undertake our work in a vacuum, of course. Decisions need to be made in the context of the broader world. And this broader world of work has changed radically in the last decade. Depending on what stage you are at, it may have changed still further by the time you take up paid employment. As the 21st century moves on, people are right to wonder how their career will progress and whether it will give them what they want.

Yet you may be sure: uncertainty and change are the order of the day. Years ago there was more certainty about how a career would progress – more inherent job security (even the phrase 'jobs for life' was used). Many organizations once had defined career paths for people and, although progress varied somewhat, once on a specific path the direction in which you would be able to go was reasonably clear. In some fields this was particularly so. Banks make a good example, yet they have changed too; many would say not for the better. They are certainly no longer an example of a safe career. Now, though this kind of prescribed career path does still exist, in general it is much less common.

There are currently few, if any, safe havens, and few, if any, organizations that seem likely to be so again in a situation where change is the norm. Organizations are always likely to be under pressure and the well-being of their employees is often a lesser goal than sheer survival.

Areas of change

All sorts of factors contribute to there being a different workplace and work culture than in the past, including:

- Organizations being under greater market and financial pressure.

- Changes in the way business and organizations operate (think of the IT revolution or international pressures, for instance).

- Lower staff numbers and more pressure on individuals.

- Reduced budgets and thus a reduced ability to fund personal development for employees.

- Changed terms of employment (for example, check out how the pension schemes offered have changed in the last few years).

- More competition between employees to succeed.

- Higher unemployment.

- A general increase in both the amount and speed of change.

- The greater likelihood of employers having to take sudden and negative action to protect themselves (such as making people redundant).

Despite all this you no doubt want to thrive, prosper and get on; and you probably want to enjoy your job while you do so. Remember that it is said that if success were easy, there would be no such thing as failure. So what is the moral? How can you ensure that you do well? The simple answer is that there is nothing you can do that will guarantee success, but there is a great deal you can do to make success more likely. High on the list and especially relevant here is developing those 'career skills' that make success in a whole range of activities more likely. They include:

- communication skills;

- interpersonal skills (not least working with other people);

- analytical thinking skills;

- problem-solving skills.

One could list many more, but key amongst them are communication skills, and several aspects, including making presentations, can be developed at university. Another aspect is written communication. Now we are not suggesting that the skill of writing a good essay and, say, writing a good business proposal or report are exactly the same, but the one certainly makes a good foundation for the other.

Skills with ongoing benefit

Skills learnt in writing essays that are useful in a business context include:

- being able to structure material well and persuasively;

- recognizing there are a variety of forms of writing, each with its own style and set of conventions that need to be followed;

- clarity of expression;

- knowing how to go about background research, and incorporate this into your own writing;

- being able to analyse and make a judgement on the writing of others;

- a good writing style, including accurate spelling and grammar.

So, time and effort spent on writing as described in this book are likely to have benefits that go well beyond creating a good academic essay. The first additional use may be in something that overlaps with your university work, yet also goes beyond it – the written aspects of finding a job. CVs, covering letters and applications are all important; indeed they make a significant difference between getting an interview (or a job) and not.

Applications in finding work and beyond

In work, and indeed outside it, the circumstances in which the quality of your writing can assist are legion. The list that follows identifies several that are important at various stages, some before you leave university and others further ahead; you may well find more:

- *Job seeking:* CVs, letters of application, addenda to application forms, correspondence with employment agencies.

- *Employment:* correspondence with your employer from day one on everything from a short (but important) e-mail to more lengthy explanations or requests.

- *Work:* documents that a job involves you in writing, such as reports or proposals and correspondence with people ranging from colleagues to customers and in formal or electronic form.

- *Networking:* keeping in touch with a range of people useful to you in job and career (even an entry on a social website needs to be clear and may need to impress).

- *Personal:* a wide range of things may be involved here from making a complaint (and seeking compensation) to applications for a loan.

TAKE CARE

It may well be that, certainly when applying for certain kinds of job, your CV should refer to your writing skills. Because it is a commonly required workplace skill it is worth spelling out your achievements in this regard as part of cataloguing your skills. The whole essay-writing process has relevance, so if your course has involved you in researching, planning and writing essays and you did well at it, then you have a significant area of achievement to mention that may expand your credentials and add power to your applications. This is even more relevant if your course has involved you in writing dissertations (see page 81), because they involve a whole project. Set out how you had to:

- work independently;

- select a topic;

- research the necessary facts and material;

- analyse and organize the material;

- plan your approach; and

- write and fine-tune to create the final document.

If you received good comments about such work it may also be worth quoting them (or a pertinent extract). This can add up to powerful stuff and may act to lift your application above others. Remember that even a small additional element can put your CV ahead of the competition.

Other opportunities here include the linking of essays or dissertations with presentations, indeed any writing task may be worth a mention: even such activities as taking minutes or writing publicity for a university society can be given a line in your CV. It all helps.

An example illustrates another aspect of all this. Sometimes even seemingly everyday chores necessitate such skills and the careful application of them makes a real difference to a variety of outcomes. Consider something you may already have to think about (and certainly will later): insurance. One of us (PF) had a travel insurance claim turned down. We won't bore you with the details – suffice to say that, though it took more than four months, when a cheque for several hundred pounds finally arrived the prime reason was believed to be the way a carefully written series of letters had been deployed.

In the workplace environment, written communications, from the humble e-mail upwards, can have even more dramatic results. Skilful writing should be fine-tuned and kept sharp because it is likely to assist you throughout your career.

Written communication in the workplace

'Writing is easy; all you do is sit staring at a blank sheet of paper until the drops of blood form on your forehead.' An author, Gene Fowler, said this about creative writing, but it might come equally to mind if you find yourself contemplating a report that needs submitting to the boss in two days' time. Most jobs come with paperwork – some of it is routine administration, some is very important. Just like presentations, written communication, that is reports, proposals, e-mails and even minutes and memos, can have a great deal hanging on them. Decisions that you want to go a particular way may be influenced not only by the quality of the thought, idea or proposal but by how the case for it is made and how it is expressed in writing. Success may also be linked to other skills, for instance that of persuasion, but that goes beyond our brief here.

Consider a report. Imagine one you might have had to read. If it is clear, well structured and descriptive; if it had a clear introduction and a succinct summary that really ties together the key issues, then it makes much more impact on you. It also makes it more likely you will actually read it all the way through; we suspect plenty of things you must read at university reinforce this point. Never forget, with an eye on your career, that everything written says something about the writer. Thus any report speaks volumes about the skill, knowledge, expertise and competence of the writer – and their clout. Yours will have to do the same.

ACTION

Consider e-mails: they are used for so many communications and, despite their informality, must be clear and do a good job of communicating. At university lecturers complain of students sending them e-mails that are, let's say, ambiguous. They are too brief and too close to texts and less formal kinds of communication; they can annoy lecturers and that is something to avoid. But good practice here will stand you in good stead later. In the workplace all communication must be clear and employers tend to be hard on those they perceive as having poor communication skills. If you view e-mails in the right light during your course, you will be in a good position once you move on to a work situation.

Ongoing development

Again, this is a skill that can be developed. As an example, one of the authors (PF), who has had a large amount of material published, readily admits that early on he had to spend time and effort to develop a workable and appropriate style.

Writing is certainly a skill that you can spend a lifetime fine-tuning. As now with your essay writing, so it should be with your business writing – regular work on it will improve it. And an effective and appropriate style will reflect well on you in your current job and in the view taken by other people regarding your future.

Back to the now ubiquitous e-mail. There is a grave likelihood of many of them being dashed off. How many do you receive that are abbreviated to the point of shoddiness – or, worse, that do not make complete sense and prompt a reply simply to gain clarification? Of course, sometimes they can be short and informal, and that's fine – but in the workplace you will always need to make clarity your first consideration, and do not allow e-mails to become less formal than the occasion, and recipient, demand. E-mails are worth a word in terms of their use right now; see box.

TAKE CARE

The question of e-mails is worth relating back to university and your communications with lecturers. If it is convenient and appropriate to communicate by e-mail (ie, only when they say it is appropriate) then make sure you do so clearly. A much-voiced complaint amongst lecturers is the need to spend time clarifying unclear messages.

A last point may provide an added incentive for you to work on your skills in this area. As your writing ability improves you get to do it faster. This saves time and is a worthwhile objective in its own right. You have only to look at the quality of much of the paperwork that circulates around many an office to see that prevailing standards often leave something to be desired; so write right and you have another essential skill that can differentiate you and make you stand out.

The key remaining thought here is that, however much of a chore writing essays may seem at a particular moment, you should remember that by working on your writing skills you are not just boosting the likelihood of getting good grades and therefore a good degree or other qualification, you are also developing a 'life skill'; one whose usefulness can extend much further.

While not all writing chrysalises will become butterflies, some students will move on to bless the day that they took a moment to get these skills right and will reap the benefit of doing so in later years.

Your notes

Afterword

And finally ...

A final thought as we come to the end. At this point, if we have met our objectives, you will be aware of two things. First, you will know the importance of having good academic essay-writing skills both throughout your time as a student and at the start of your career, with the latter being adapted in various ways in the workplace. The time it takes to write a good essay in the style and form that academia demands may be little more than (or the same as) what is needed to write a lacklustre one, but what it will do for you is so much more.

Secondly, you will know something of how to go about acquiring and deploying suitable writing skills. The process of getting to grips with this is not complex. Some time and effort are certainly necessary and every stage, from how you view a question to research and 'getting it down on paper', needs care but each stage of the process is essentially manageable. It is something best tackled early in your course so that you can benefit from being able to create good essays and do so more easily throughout your time at university.

Whilst not wanting to devalue anything said in the course of the book (success is largely in the detail), one thing is sure to help. All writers are commended to read widely. The essayist Richard Steele said: 'Reading is to the mind what exercise is to the body.' He was probably talking about the content, the power of reading to inform, but it is a truism that exposure to writing, particularly if you take note, can progressively teach you a good deal about everything from grammar to style. Every kind of reading can help: a novel may contain powerful language and description and something like popular science writing can help with the process of explaining difficult ideas in a comprehensible way.

Your course itself may involve a good deal of reading. Mark Connelly, who kindly wrote our Foreword, tells us that students studying history on the kind of course with which he is concerned are often surprised at the number of books they must read before they get to the final exam. So opportunities abound in addition to any recreational reading you may undertake. And it may help to read books about language and writing. Reference books are mentioned earlier in the text, but there are other books that are interesting and entertaining and fun to read, including:

Radio 4's John Humphreys' book, *Lost for Words* (Hodder & Stoughton).

Lynne Truss's *Eats, Shoots & Leaves*, which became a bestseller and is surely the most amusing guide to punctuation ever written.

Strictly English by Simon Heffer (who acts as writing style guru for the *Daily Telegraph*) is a longer review of written language; also very readable.

English our English by the late Keith Waterhouse is probably the best of all: a short, impassioned treatise on how to write effectively. Sadly and inexplicably this is out of print, though there are copies on Amazon for just a penny (and on other such websites too no doubt).

In addition, more routine books could also be useful. Writer's Digest Books publishes a whole list of books for writers, some concerned with specific genres such as fiction, others – such as *Write Tight* by William Brohaugh (subtitled, *How to keep your prose sharp, focused and concise*) – focus on specific techniques useful in this context. Books designed for people other than students may also be useful, for instance *Effective Business Writing* by Patrick Forsyth (Kogan Page).

Reading adds to the process of acquiring the habits of good writing, which can develop over time. And habit is the factor that ultimately reduces the chore aspect of good writing. You always need to think, you also need to check (we have lost track of how many times we read over the text of this book before sending it to the publishers!), indeed good checking, let us restate, is essential. Poor checking can so easily mean something is marked down, its effectiveness diluted and mistakes included that could have been avoided easily. Examples abound and some have been quoted already; a final one comes from a university website, which states that students should enter a password of 'between 7 and 8 characters'. Even those studying mathematics might wonder what this means. But good writing is possible and if you achieve it then it makes a real difference.

Having said that, an awareness of language, indeed actively developing an awareness of language, helps. Let us end with a teaser – a little exercise to reinforce our
last point, and perhaps prompt you to action. Take a moment to read the following
paragraph and see if you can answer the question it poses.

As you scan this short paragraph, try to spot what is unusual about it. Half an hour is normal
for many to find a solution that is both logical and satisfactory to its originator. I do not say that
anything is 'wrong' about it, simply that it is unusual. You may want to study its grammatical
construction to find a solution, but that is not a basis of its abnormality, nor is its lack of any
information, logical points or conclusion. If you work in communication you may find that an
aid to solving this particular conundrum. It is not about anagrams, synonyms, antonyms or
acrostics, but it is unusual. So, why is that?

The answer is shown on page 137. This is only a bit of fun, but it makes an important
point: to write well you must read. The more interest you take in language, the more
you notice what makes it good or bad, then the more it will influence you. There is no
harm in copying examples of style and approach that appeal to you, nor is there in
adapting and tweaking things for your own purpose.

For instance, we noticed only recently the device of the very short sentence turned
into one word sentences to create added emphasis. It. Really. Works. And, like much
else, provided it is not overused, it adds to the power to make the point you want.
And, while so much contributes – research, analysis, planning and all the elements
mentioned – making a considered point and making it well can without doubt
help you towards an excellent essay in suitable (academic) style and ultimately to a
successful graduation.

Acknowledgements

The author of many books, I have also worked successfully in collaboration with a number of writers in the past; doing so can be something that requires effort and organization for both those involved. But this collaboration has been special, and thus I have penned these brief paragraphs solo.

As the lead author of two co-authored works with Jacqueline Connelly (this one and the earlier *The Study Skills Guide*) I must thank her here again for her involvement in this assignment. I may have set the project up, but she again made it possible; she worked tirelessly to complete her part of the material and brought to the whole text invaluable experience, knowledge and insight of the content. Her direct university experience both as a student and a manager literally saw this book to fruition and ensured it truly addresses the real student experience in a practical and helpful way.

As with the first book, her patience in face of my impatience and her nit-picking attention to university workings and terminology made her an admirable collaborator. Thank you so much Jacqui.

Finally, thanks are due to all those who assisted with the example material in Chapter 6: they are listed in the chapter and will not be repeated, but they contributed greatly. Thanks also to those at the publisher Kogan Page who thought to include us in its growing list of titles designed to give practical help to students.

Patrick Forsyth

Answer: the answer to the little conundrum on page 136 is that the paragraph of text in the box that poses the question is written without the use of the letter e. This is the most commonly occurring letter of the alphabet in English and avoiding it inevitably produces a slightly odd feel to the text.

Index